C000024685

THE LORD'S SUPPER IN HUMAN HANDS

WHO SHOULD ADMINISTER?

EDITORS
PETER G. BOLT, MARK D. THOMPSON, ROBERT TONG

The Lord's Supper in Human Hands
© 2008 belongs to the individual authors of the essays, or the editors, as indicated. The views expressed in the various essays, or by the editors, are not necessarily shared in their entirety by all other authors.

Australian Church Record
(ACN 000 071 438)
PO Box 218
Camperdown NSW 1450
www.australianchurchrecord.net

Distributed in Australia by:
Australian Church Record

Distributed in the United Kingdom by:
The Latimer Trust
PO Box 26685
London N14 4XQ
www.latimertrust.org

Anglican Church League can to contacted at: www.acl.asn.au

National Library of Australia Cataloguing-in-Publication entry

Title:	The Lord's Supper in human hands : who should administer? / editors, Peter G. Bolt, Mark D. Thompson, Robert Tong.
Edition:	1st ed.
ISBN:	9780980376951 (pbk.)
Subjects:	Lord's Supper—Anglican Church of Australia. Lord's Supper—Anglican Communion. Lord's Supper—Lay administration—Anglican Church of Australia. Lord's Supper—Lay celebration—Anglican Church of Australia.

Other Authors/Contributors:
Bolt, Peter, 1958–
Thompson, Mark (Mark Donald)
Tong, Robert.

Dewey Number:
264.03036

Cover design and typesetting by Lankshear Design Pty Ltd. Phone: 02 9868 7044.
Printed in Australia by Ligare Pty Ltd. Phone: 02 9533 2555.

Contents

Introduction

This little book is intended as a brief introduction to the discussion of Lay Presidency or Lay Administration of the Lord's Supper. It is a discussion that has been going on within the Anglican Diocese of Sydney for more than thirty years, producing numerous reports, position papers, recommendations to the synod and drafts of legislation. Those involved have always been concerned to explain as clearly and as widely as possible why they believe a move in this direction is important and necessary. These debates have been extensive, and engagement with the objections of those inside and outside the diocese has been both ongoing and profitable. Nevertheless, the need to rehearse the explanations that have been given, for a new generation of Sydney synodspeople and for our brothers and sisters in other places, has become increasingly obvious.

We have tried to gather in these pages the essence of the discussion about whether the absolute prohibition against anyone except the priest (or presbyter) administering the Lord's Supper should continue or be removed for theological reasons. We have deliberately avoided providing all the details. These can be obtained from the various reports to the Sydney Synod. Rather, we have attempted a digest of theological, historical and legal material, which together will give an accurate picture of why successive Sydney synods have voiced their support for the removal of the prohibition. We hope it will also show that this question has surfaced in other places and at other times and so is far from an eccentric preoccupation of one small group of people.

The proposal to allow authorised deacons and laypeople to administer the Lord's Supper within a Christian congregation has never been an attempt to undermine our Anglican heritage. As the address by John Woodhouse included in this volume makes clear, it is a change in order to stay the same. In order to preserve the theological inheritance of all Anglicans, this change should be made. Thomas Cranmer, the architect of Anglican polity and the principal author of its foundational liturgical document, the *Book of Common Prayer*, envisaged the necessity of such changes in order to preserve a clear testimony to biblical truth in the churches.

It is of particular concern to us that in the current crisis within the Anglican Communion, some have drawn a parallel between the proposal to remove the prohibition on all but the presbyter administering the Supper, and the revision of biblical teaching on human sexuality in some quarters that would endorse homosexual practice. However, the difference between these two issues could not be more stark. The Bible is entirely silent on who should administer the Lord's Supper. The conventional Anglican prohibition has no root whatsoever in Scripture. In contrast, the biblical prohibition against homosexual behaviour—indeed on all sexual intimacy outside the context of the life-long union of a man and woman in marriage—is both unambiguous and constant throughout the Old and New Testaments. It may be true that both issues have proven to be controversial. But placing them in any kind of parallel neglects the simple fact that, in the light of contemporary cultural values, with regard to issues of human sexuality which are clearly addressed in the Scriptures, one attempts to revise that teaching; whereas, on the contrary, our present concern arises from a determination to remain faithful to the teaching of Scripture, while dealing with something it is silent about.

This volume begins with a slightly reworked address by John

Woodhouse, Principal of Moore College and a member of many of the committees which reported on the issue to the Sydney Synod throughout the 1980s and 1990s. His is an overview of the case in favour of removing the prohibition. Mark Thompson, head of Theology at Moore College, provides a digest of the theological arguments that have been used and an outline of the responses that have been made to various theological objections to the move. Peter Bolt, the head of New Testament at Moore College, provides two chapters, one an overview of the history of the debate in Sydney and the other which sets the question in a global context. Glenn Davies, Bishop of North Sydney, provides material in support of diaconal administration of the Lord's Supper. Robert Tong, a solicitor, lecturer in law and a longstanding member of the Sydney Standing Committee, has contributed some concluding observations. The bibliography lists all the major reports of relevance to Sydney's long journey with this issue.

The discussion in Sydney—and beyond—on this issue has been extensive. That does not mean, however, that all have yet had access to the arguments in favour of a change in our practice, a change in order to stay the same. Our prayer is that this little volume might fill that need and explain why the Diocese of Sydney has supported this measure repeatedly over the last thirty years.

Peter Bolt
Mark Thompson
Robert Tong

I

Lay Administration
of the Lord's Supper:
A change to stay the same[1]

JOHN WOODHOUSE

Evangelicals must be committed to practicing what they preach. We cannot be content with practices which obscure or distort the gospel. That is why many Anglican evangelicals today are urging the removal of the prohibition which restricts the administration of the Lord's Supper to ordained priests.

The prohibition has no basis in Scripture. Indeed it is remarkable that a role, which is not even mentioned in the New Testament, should have become so important in the minds of many. There are some who suggest that a change in this matter, on which Scripture is completely silent, is more radical than any of the changes in church belief and practice over the last 400 years. Article VI brings a truer perspective:

> Holy Scripture containeth all things necessary to salvation: so that whatsoever is not read therein, nor may be proved thereby, is not required of any man, that it should be believed as an article of the Faith, or be thought requisite or necessary to salvation.

The problem perceived by many evangelicals is that the prohibition of lay persons from ever administering the Lord's Supper suggests to many in our churches (and to many outside our churches) that:

(a) there is something about an ordained priest that gives him/her the power to pray the prayer of consecration—a power which a lay person cannot have;

(b) higher qualifications are needed for the administration of the Lord's Supper than for preaching the Word of God—lay persons can often do the latter, but never the former;

(c) the validity of the Supper depends somehow on the person administering it—a priest (*any* priest) is needed to make the occasion authentic;

(d) ordination has more to do with the Sacrament than with preaching—a priest can share his preaching ministry with competent lay persons, but not his ministry of administering the Lord's Supper; and

(e) a priest is *essential* to the conduct of the Lord's Supper—though not essential for any other event in church life.

In each of these ways the practice of absolutely prohibiting a non-priest from administering the Lord's Supper contradicts, or at the very least obscures, the gospel we preach.

A change to stay the same

There are times when you have to change in order to stay the same. In order to remain true to fundamental principles, there are times when the forms, which express those fundamentals, must change. Forms, which performed one function at one time and in one context, must be open to change if that same function is not to be obscured and hampered at another time and in another context. *The Book of Common Prayer* itself insists that forms should change 'according to the various exigencies of times and occasions'[2]:

'There was never any thing by the wit of man so well devised, or so sure established, which in continuance of time hath not been corrupted.'[3]

The Book of Common Prayer recognises that there are things that 'at the first were of godly intent and purpose devised, and yet at length turned to vanity and superstition'.[4]

It is the contention of this paper that the absolute prohibition of any person who is not an ordained priest from administering the Lord's Supper was 'at the first of godly intent and purpose devised', but 'yet at length [has] turned to vanity and superstition'.

It is helpful to distinguish the prohibition itself (which I will call a 'form') from its effects ('function'). The function of the prohibition today is very different from its function in the 16th and 17th centuries.

Consider the restrictions that surrounded public ministry in 1662. *The Book of Common Prayer* envisaged no lay ministry of the Word, or of the Lord's Supper. However:

> It appertaineth to the office of a Deacon [...] to assist the Priest in Divine Service, and specially when he ministereth the holy Communion, and to help him in the distribution thereof, and to read holy Scriptures and Homilies in the Church [...] and to preach if he be admitted thereto by the Bishop.[5]

It is not clear how extensive the involvement of the deacon in the Lord's Supper might have been. The rubrics of the *Order for the Administration of the Lord's Supper* specifically indicate that it was to be the priest who said/read:

The Lord's Prayer
The Collect
The Ten Commandments
The Collect for the Queen
The Epistle
The Gospel
The Offertory Sentence(s)

The general Prayer for 'the whole state of Christ's Church militant
    here in earth'
The Exhortation (at the time of the celebration of the Communion)
The call to repentance
The Absolution (said by the Bishop, if present)
The comfortable words
'It is meet, right, and our bounded duty [...]'
The prayer of humble access
The Prayer of Consecration
The Lord's Prayer
The Blessing (said by the Bishop, if present)

It is particularly interesting to note that the Prayer of Consecration is one of many items, which, according to the rubrics, are to be said by the priest. The 1662 *Act of Uniformity* made it clear that only those who had been episcopally ordained priest may 'consecrate and administer the holy sacrament of the Lord's Supper'. However, it is now commonly accepted in many parts of the Anglican Communion that a person other than the priest (a deacon or an authorised lay person) may say/ read several of the above items, but never the Prayer of Consecration. It is not clear why the rubric to that prayer has popularly been given more weight than the others. Restricting that prayer to the priest, except on the same grounds that virtually the whole liturgy is restricted to him, has no basis in *The Book of Common Prayer*.

In 1662 the prohibition against non-priests from administering the Lord's Supper, expressed in the *Act of Uniformity*, was part and parcel of the restriction of all public ministry to the clergy. Only clergy had any part in the public ministry of the Word of God and the Sacrament of the Lord's Supper. There is no concept in *The Book of Common Prayer* of a lay person ever taking any part in the public liturgy of the church. Those who appeal to 'Anglican Order' must be very clear that in 1662 'Anglican Order' excluded lay persons from any part in public ministry. Certainly they were excluded from preaching, but also from leading Morning or Evening Prayer, reading the Scriptures in church, and so on.

In 1662 there was a hedge around *all* public ministry of Word and Sacrament. It was a big hedge. And it would be appropriate to describe this as a form with a 'godly intent and purpose'. In a day of widespread illiteracy, limited theological understanding —certainly among the laity—and a recently reformed church, the purpose and function of this restriction was to guard the public ministry of the gospel from corruption. It was a kind of quality control.

It is important to understand that in the 16th and 17th centuries in the Church of England, the fact that only priests could administer the Lord's Supper was not based on the idea that only priests, by virtue of their episcopal ordination, had the power to administer the Supper. Even a casual reading of Thomas Cranmer on the Lord's Supper will dispel that idea. Neither was it some concept of the 'president of the community' who was the right person to 'preside' at the Lord's Supper. That is a novel idea in Anglicanism, and has never been the practice. It is not that the Rector (or equivalent) must do it. There has never been an objection to assistant priests, or visiting priests administering the Sacrament. The issue in the 16th and 17th centuries was quality control. Only priests could do it. But not necessarily the Rector. And the same rule applied to *all* public ministry in church.

Canon 56 of the Canons of 1603 illustrates this last point. This canon envisages a minister who has 'cure and charge of souls', and who may 'chiefly attend to preaching', having 'a Curate under him to execute the other duties which are to be performed for him in the Church'. These duties included the administration of the Lord's Supper. The canon prescribes that such a minister must himself read the Divine Service and administer the Lord's Supper at least twice a year! On all other occasions 'the Curate under him' may perform this duty for him. There is no suggestion that the Lord's Supper should normally be administered by the minister 'that hath cure and charge of souls'.

Too much of the modern debate has departed far from a reformed understanding of ministry and sacraments. Thomas Cranmer discussed the distinction between priests and lay people in relation to the Lord's Supper in terms that are relevant to the present debate:

> Therefore Christ made no such difference between the priest and the layman, that the priest should make oblation and sacrifice of Christ for the layman, and eat the Lord's Supper from him, all alone and distribute and apply it as him liketh. Christ made no such difference; but the difference that is between the priest and the layman in this matter is only in the ministration; that the priest, as a common minister [i.e. servant] of the Church, doth minister and distribute the Lord's Supper unto other, and other receive it at his hands. [...] As in a prince's house the officers and ministers [i.e. servants] prepare the table, and yet other, as well as they, eat the meat and drink the drink; so do the priests and ministers prepare the Lord's Supper, read the Gospel, and rehearse Christ's words; but *all the people* say thereto, Amen; *all* remember Christ's death, all give thanks to God, *all* repent and offer themselves an oblation to Christ, *all* take him for their Lord and Saviour, and spiritually feed upon him; and in token thereof, they eat the bread and drink the wine in his mystical [i.e. symbolic] Supper.[6]

Cranmer went to great lengths to play down the significance of the role of the priest at the Supper, and to emphasise that all that matters as we eat and drink together in remembrance of Christ's death, we all do together. The priest, like a servant in a king's house, prepares the Supper, and serves both the Word and the symbol of the Word. It is clear that Cranmer not only never did, but he never would, call the priest's role in the Lord's Supper 'presidency'.

However, for the purpose of guarding the public ministry of Word and sacrament, it was *all* restricted to the clergy: essentially to priests, with some assistance from deacons.

While that wide restriction in the 16th and 17th centuries can be regarded as 'of godly intent and purpose devised', that does not mean that it can or should be retained at the end of the 20th century. Today we are blessed with many gifted and highly educated, theologically qualified lay people. While oversight of congregations is still rightly entrusted to fully trained and recognised ordained persons, competent lay persons now share in the public ministry of the Word, and of prayer, and indeed often play some public role in the ministry of the Lord's Supper (such as assisting in distribution, or leading some of the prayers). This development has been largely uncontroversial and beneficial to us all.

Therefore the form ('Anglican order', if you like) has already changed radically, for the very good reason that today to restrict all public ministry to the clergy only would be to *rob* the church of much quality ministry. To insist that this further change is objectionable, because it is 'contrary to Anglican order' fails to appreciate the enormous changes that have already (and properly) taken place.

However a remnant of the old general prohibition remains. One aspect of public ministry still has that hedge about it. The hedge made sense when it surrounded all public ministry and, so to speak, protected it from ignorant and incompetent lay persons. But the hedge makes no sense when it is left around only one aspect of public ministry, and protects it from highly competent and knowledgable lay persons who share in church leadership in every other conceivable way under the oversight of the Rector.

Today the prohibition no longer serves its original function, and indeed works against the very theology which gave rise to it. It has, in the words of *The Book of Common Prayer*, 'at length turned to vanity and superstition'. Go back to the Reformation, and you will not find the ministry of the sacrament separated off from the ministry of the word like this, as though a higher qualification is needed for administering the Lord's Supper than for preaching. Indeed, if anything, you will only find the reverse. Martin Luther wrote 'the man to whom has been committed the office of preaching has committed to him the highest office in the Christian Church. He may also baptize, say mass [...]'.[7]

To remove the absolute prohibition that has become part of Anglican church life would be to express an understanding of both ministry and the sacraments that is closer to our Anglican formularies.

This is one of those times when it is important to change in order to stay the same.

Not 'presidency'

Some confusion has come into the discussion of lay involvement with the Sacrament of the Lord's Supper, by the use of the term 'presidency'. The word is unhelpful for a number of reasons.

Firstly, 'president' is not a term found in the New Testament or *The Book of Common Prayer*, and its first known relevant use (by Justin Martyr in his First Apology) seems to be a reference to the regular head of the congregation in terms that would be understood by outsiders.[8] *The Book of Common Prayer* speaks of 'ministering' or 'administering' the Sacrament, a rather different concept.

Secondly, it has become usual to use the term 'president' to refer to the person who leads the people on a particular liturgical occasion (such as the Lord's Supper). The confusion arises because others (probably including Justin Martyr) refer to the 'president of the community', an ongoing role, not restricted to any particular occasion. The matter under consideration has been whether the only person who can 'preside' (in the former sense) is the 'president of the community'. Some have suggested that any 'presidency' exercised by a lay person will undermine the 'presidency' of the priest. This can be more clearly considered if different terms are used for the two concepts.

Thirdly, it is worth noting that even now a lay person can (and probably does occasionally) 'preside' (in an ordinary sense of the word) at the Lord's Supper quite legally, and without controversy. If, say, in the absence of the Rector, a lay person welcomes the congregation, and, leads them in the first part of the liturgy (the 'Ante-Communion'), but invites a visiting priest to say the Prayer of Consecration, and to distribute the elements with the lay person's help, many would regard the lay person as the 'president' of that gathering on that occasion.

Fourthly, lay administration of the Lord's Supper should acknowledge the oversight that rightly belongs to the priest to whose 'cure and charge' the people have been committed. The Rector remains the 'president' of the congregation, but the particular service, at the 'president's' direction, is carried out by a lay person. Like all lay (and diaconal) ministry, this ministry would be 'assisting the priest'. The term 'presidency' for 'administration' tends to obscure this fact.

Fifthly, in the administration of the Lord's Supper the focus is not on the minister, but (as Cranmer emphasised) on the corporate act of remembering the Lord's death through the total activity of the thanksgiving, distributing and eating together. The term 'presidency' tends to give too much weight to the role of the minister.

What about our 'order'?

Some who agree that there are no theological objections to lay administration of the Lord's Supper, nevertheless object that such a 'novelty' would be contrary to Anglican 'order'. 'Order' is a word used in a number of different ways in this debate. Sometimes 'order' means 'order' as opposed to chaos! What would the proposed change do to our relationships with other Anglicans, and to our relationships with other denominations, particularly the Roman Catholics?

It should be remembered that the Anglican Communion already lives with considerable diversity of opinion and practice. With good will and respect for sincerely held convictions, there is no reason for this change to be of greater concern than other differences. Indeed to suggest that this is the change which we *cannot* make would imply that what binds Anglicans together is some common sacramental theology—and that a theology which few evangelicals could endorse. These remarks apply with even more force to our relationships with the Roman Catholic denomination.

By 'order' others mean the ordering of ministry in the Anglican Church. Specifically there is commitment to the three 'orders' of bishop, priest, and deacon.

To think that lay administration of the Lord's Supper will be more damaging to these orders than lay preaching has been suggests that ordination is more about the Sacraments than it is about preaching. This view cannot be supported from either the New Testament or *The Book of Common Prayer*.

In *The Book of Common Prayer*, ordination to the priesthood authorises a person to oversee a congregation: 'how great a treasure [the sheep of Christ] is *committed to your charge*', 'the people *committed to your charge*', 'the people *committed to your cure and charge*', 'them that are or shall be committed to your charge'. This oversight is certainly exercised through preaching the Word of God and ministering the Sacraments, but just as a person may be competent to preach sermons from time to time, without all the training and gifts necessary for full time pastoral oversight of the congregation, so such a person may be fully competent to administer the Lord's Supper from time to time, without either being ready to be ordained, or threatening the significance of ordination.[9]

Still others use 'order' as a way of referring to custom. Some feel that it is just too great a change from the way in which Anglicans have always done things and the practice which *The Book of Common Prayer* prescribes. Some may like to call such custom 'tradition'. This is misleading. Theologically the 'tradition' of the Christian Church is the Scriptures. Custom, however ancient, must never be elevated to the level of 'tradition'.

Quite clearly what is being proposed is a change in our customary ways. It is yet another change from the ways prescribed in *The Book of Common Prayer*. However to object to this change, but to accept lay preaching and many other changes to the ways of the church in the 16th and 17th centuries is arbitrary, and unjustified.

So long as there are sound theological objections to our present 'order', appeals to maintain that 'order' (in any of these senses) are not compelling, and amount to merely unprincipled conservatism.

The place of the Lord's Supper in church life

The Lord's Supper is an important occasion to which 'all such as shall be religiously and devoutly disposed'[10] should come, and 'the people negligent to come'[11] should be exhorted 'that ye will not refuse to come thereto, being so lovingly called and bidden by God himself.'[12] The reasons given in the second Exhortation in the Order for the Administration of the Lord's Supper are that to refuse to come when God himself has bidden you is shameful, and a neglect of duty. 'Sore punishments hang over your heads for the same; when ye wilfully abstain from the Lord's Table, and separate from your brethren ...'

The proposal to allow persons other than a priest to administer the Lord's Supper has led some to reconsider the place of the Sacrament in the life of the church. Some have found support for the present prohibition in a notion that the Lord's Supper is a complete occasion in which the whole community is involved, and where the appropriate 'president' must be the one with pastoral oversight (the priest). This reasoning rests on two fictions.

Fiction 1: that the administration of the Lord's Supper is restricted to the one with pastoral oversight. This (as was pointed out earlier) is not, and has never been, the case. An assistant minister who is a priest, or a visiting priest can, and frequently does, administer the Sacrament. An assistant minister who is a deacon, or a lay person, cannot.

Fiction 2: that the Lord's Supper is the essential expression of the whole community's life. This, too, seems to be a novel invention to support a custom that has arisen without any such rationale. *The Book of Common Prayer* has no such notion: 'Every parishioner shall communicate at least three times in the year'.[13] Only three persons need to be present. If a sick person 'be not able to come to the Church'[14] the Lord's Supper can be administered in the sick man's house. In special circumstances a minister may communicate with a sick person with no one else present. *The Book of Common Prayer* does not suggest that the

Lord's Supper is *the* expression of the community's life.

Of course there are occasions where it is most appropriate for the one entrusted with the 'cure of souls' in that place to administer the Sacrament, just as there are occasions when it is most appropriate for the Rector to preach. However to extend the argument to say that the Lord's Supper is *always* such an occasion cannot be sustained.

Conclusion

Change is always difficult, particularly significant change. Change will nearly always be resisted. Change causes unease among some. So we need to take great care with change. But because change will often feel uncomfortable at the start, even change that is called for by sound principles requires a bit of courage. I have tried to work out why some people are uneasy about *this* change.

I have a theory. When you are clear about why you do what you do, then you can be relaxed about changing the forms when this is necessary and helpful.

For example: evangelicals are generally pretty clear about the purpose of preaching in church. The sermon serves the function of teaching or proclaiming the Word of God; of enabling God's people (and others) to hear God's Word. Since we are clear about the function of preaching, we have had little difficulty coping with a radical change to the form, namely allowing certain lay persons to preach. We can see that nowadays that does not necessarily damage the purpose of preaching. Because we understand the *purpose* clearly, we have no difficulty accepting proper changes to the *form*, so that it can function even better. Indeed I think that most of us can see that to insist that today's preaching be surrounded by the same restrictions, and take the same form as in the Church of England in the 16th and 17th centuries would today be to hinder the very purpose for which preaching was shaped in the 16th century.

However when you are less clear about why you do what you do, you can find yourself focusing on the form, and thinking that the form matters *in itself*. I take it that that is why we hear people saying 'It's against Anglican *order*.' But it can only be 'against' Anglican order if you think that the form is unchangeable. Then lay preaching would be against Anglican order. Lay persons reading Morning Prayer would be against Anglican order. Lay persons taking any part whatsoever in public liturgy would be against Anglican order. But *The Book of Common Prayer* rejects the notion that forms are unchangeable.

I believe that because we are much less clear about the *function* of administering the Lord's Supper than we are about the function of preaching, we feel that this is a more dramatic change in our way of doing things than allowing lay preachers was.

But we are less clear for good reason. The role of the priest in the Lord's Supper, as Cranmer insisted, is not itself important. Of all the ministries mentioned in the New Testament, there is not a word about who should take the leading role at the Lord's Supper, not a word to elders or anyone else that they should do it. That role is relatively unimportant since the focus is not on what that person does, but on the corporate act of remembering the Lord's death together.

Once that is clear, I believe we can see that the change in form will be good and will help people to understand the gospel better. The prohibition as it stands is one of those things that, in the words of *The Book of Common Prayer,* 'at the first was of godly intent and purpose devised, and yet at length has turned to vanity and superstition'. If that is so, it *must* be removed, for the sake of the gospel. I suspect that it will turn out to like a bit like a church I attended in the 1960's, where the priest did *everything*, except take up the collection. And that was only done by the wardens. It was unthinkable that anyone else would take up the collection, or that a lay person would read the lesson. We probably thought it was illegal, or at least contrary to church 'order'. Gradually people came to accept that it was not only *legal*, but it was *good* for unnecessary and theologically groundless taboos to be removed from our church life.

It helped us (and, importantly, others) to understand the truth of the gospel better. So will the removal of this one.

ENDNOTES

1   This paper is a revision and expansion of a speech given to the Synod of the Diocese of Sydney in October, 1994, moving the second reading of a bill for an ordinance enabling lay persons and deacons to be authorised to administer the Lord's Supper. Readers will note that aspects of the original genre have not been entirely eliminated.

2   From *The Preface*.

3   From *Concerning the Service of the Church*.

4   From *Of Ceremonies: why some be abolished, and some retained*.

5   From *The Form and Manner of Making of Deacons*.

6   *A Defence of the True and Catholick Doctrine of the Sacrament*, Book V, chapter XI ('The difference between the priest and the layman'). Emphases added.

7   Luther, 'The Right and Power of a Christian Congregation', 84.

8   See Robinson, 'Presidency and Assistance in Ministering Word and Sacrament: A Note'.

9   [Editors' note: It is interesting to note that when it was suggested that the laity could assist at the Lord's Supper, it was felt that this would threaten the role of the deacon, and force a redefinition of that ministry. As lay assistants became more common and widespread, this threat fell away. The threat is now being felt in regard to the priest's role. Although this helpfully clarifies what the priest is— and is not— all about, there is no need for priests to feel threatened by the advent of lay administration.]

10   From the first Exhortation in *The Order for the Administration of the Lord's Supper*.

11   From the rubric preceding the second Exhortation.

12   From the second Exhortation.

13   From the rubrics at the end of *The Order for the Administration of the Lord's Supper*.

14   From the rubric at the beginning of *The Communion of the Sick*.

2

Lay Administration: The Theological Considerations

MARK D. THOMPSON

Who may administer the Lord's Supper in a Christian congregation? Must the person who does so be episcopally ordained? These questions have received careful and deliberate attention in the Anglican Diocese of Sydney since at least Synod Resolution 9 from 1977. The impetus for such extended conversations and consultations in Sydney has always been theological rather than pragmatic, something that has not always been understood elsewhere. The conclusions reached have also been determined by theological considerations. The 1993 Sydney Doctrine Commission report is representative:

> In summary, there are no sound doctrinal objections to, and there are significant doctrinal reasons for, lay presidency at the Lord's Supper. There are also sound reasons based on our received Anglican order for allowing lay presidency. In the light of this the continued prohibition of lay presidency at the Lord's Supper does not seem justifiable theologically. Since church practice ought to conform to sound doctrine, practical problems related to the introduction of lay presidency ought to be dealt with, but should

not constitute an obstacle to reform motivated by theological truth.[1]

Two preliminary observations about terminology will aid the clarity of all that follows. The first is that this chapter seeks to use the term 'administration' rather than 'presidency' except when quoting from one of the numerous reports on the subject. As a committee report from 1994 argued, the use of the term 'presidency' leads to confusion between a particular liturgical function and the ongoing role of oversight in the congregation.[2]

Secondly, the language of 'priest', though it has been long used in Anglican discussion, is itself a source of additional confusion. To many contemporary ears it suggests a sacerdotalism that the Reformation explicitly rejected. For this reason, Sydney synod has preferred to use 'presbyter', a term closer to the biblical language, to refer to an elder in a congregation who has been episcopally ordained. In what follows the expression 'non-presbyter' is also frequently used, and the intention has consistently been to include both deacons and those traditionally (but problematically) referred to as 'laypeople' in that expression.[3]

As the chronology of the discussion makes clear,[4] time and again the Sydney Synod and its various committees and commissions have concluded that the Lord's Supper need not be administered only by persons who have been episcopally ordained. The aim of this chapter is to outline as succinctly as possible the doctrinal reasons that have led to this conclusion, as well as to acknowledge and respond to the doctrinal objections which others have raised. At each point reference is made to the reports where these reasons have been explored in more detail. It is certainly true that the debates have often ranged wider than doctrinal issues to include arguments from tradition and history, as well as legal and constitutional matters. However, these have always been seen as secondary considerations, which ought not to determine the matter, and so they are not included in this chapter. This issue is first and foremost a theological matter. That is why over the last thirty years there has been substantial agreement that this issue needs to be decided on theological grounds.

It will be useful if we attempt to provide the sharpest possible focus on the issue being debated. The argument *for* administration of the Lord's Supper by non-presbyters is an argument *against* an absolute prohibition. Successive synods, committees and commissions have argued that maintaining such a prohibition—one which has no biblical warrant whatsoever—is not just pragmatically undesirable but has serious negative theological consequences. Amongst the most important of these is the way this prohibition places an inordinate importance upon a role, which is not even mentioned in the New Testament.

Putting the theological case

The theological rationale for the administration of the Lord's Supper by those who have not been episcopally ordained arises from the nature of life in the light of the gospel, the nature of Christian ministry and the nature of the Lord's Supper itself.

The nature of the Christian life

- **The place of the Bible in the life of the Christian.** As God's word to us, the teaching of Scripture makes known the person and purposes of God in the gospel of Jesus Christ and directs us in response to that gospel. Nothing may bind the Christian conscience more tightly than the word of God. Where Scripture is silent, or where it explicitly declares a matter to be indifferent, freedom is more appropriate than command or prohibition. In this light, it is particularly significant that the Bible does not address the question of who should administer the Lord's Supper. Since this is the case, we are prompted to ask 'How absolute can a prohibition be on a subject about which Scripture is silent before that prohibition supplants the final authority of Scripture?'

- **The priesthood of all believers.** 'The kingdom of Christ [...] is not limited by the restrictions which fetter other societies, political or religious. It has no sacred days or seasons, no special sanctuaries, because every time and every place alike are holy. Above all it has no sacerdotal system. It interposes no sacrificial tribal class between God and man, by whose intervention alone God is reconciled and man forgiven. Each individual member holds personal communion with the divine Head.'[5] The Christian presbyter does not stand between God and his people but amid and alongside them as one of those exercising particular gifts for the benefit of the congregation. Administering the sacrament is certainly not a 'priestly' function in any sense. Christ Jesus himself is our only 'priest' since he is the only necessary mediator between human beings and God. A prohibition against non-presbyters administering the Lord's Supper is difficult to reconcile with this reality.

- **The ministry of all believers.** Alongside the priesthood of all believers, the Bible teaches the ministry of all believers. The Holy Spirit has gifted each believer in order that the congregation might grow in maturity and Christlikeness. A critical way in which pastor-teachers serve the congregation is by equipping other members for their own ministries (Eph. 4:11–12). One such ministry is leadership, which is exercised by those members whose gifts of experience and maturity commend them to the congregation. Administering the Lord's Supper in the congregation is a proper expression of such gifts.[6] The congregation should be able to authorise its own leaders, whether episcopally ordained or not.

The nature of Christian ministry

- **The responsibilities of presbyters in the New Testament.** There is no reference to administration of the Lord's Supper in the New Testament passages, which speak of the qualifications and responsibilities of presbyters. This does not necessarily mean presbyters were not involved in this way, but if from the beginning this activity was restricted to them we would expect it to feature in these passages. The silence may well suggest that a disproportionate prominence has been accrued to this function since the apostolic period.[7]

- **The essence of ordained ministry.** When 'lay people' are permitted to share in every form of ministry except one in the regular meetings of the congregation, the impression can be given that the prohibited thing is the essence of ordained ministry.[8] It suggests that ordination as a presbyter has more do with administering the sacrament than with preaching the word of God. This becomes much more than a mere suggestion when our current practice allows a presbyter to share his preaching ministry with competent non-presbyters but he may not share his ministry of administering the Lord's Supper. In such circumstances a sacerdotal view of the presbyterate is difficult to avoid. In contrast, the New Testament would lead us to conclude that at the heart of Christian eldership is a responsibility for the congregation, which is far more extensive than a particular liturgical function.

- **A rejection of all that might suggest a sacrificial priesthood.** The biblical doctrines of justification by faith alone, of the person of Christ and his atoning death, of the Word of God, and of the apostolic mission, together lead both to the rejection of sacerdotalism and to an insistence on the unity of word and sacrament. The presbyter is neither a sacrificing priest (the one Christian sacrifice has been made by the one Christian priest, Jesus Christ, on the cross) nor a dispenser of 'sacramental grace' (since grace is not a substance dispensed but God's undeserved favour on the basis of which we are united to Christ by faith). The prohibition against all but the presbyter administering the Lord's Supper at best creates confusion at these crucial points and at worst compromises them.[9]

- **The practice of visiting 'celebrants' reinforces this misunderstanding.** Where a congregation is obliged to ask a presbyter who is not a regular member to join them in order that they might share in the Lord's Supper, this reinforces a sacerdotal view of the presbyterate, which is contrary to Scripture. It suggests a special endowment on the part of the presbyter, which means that only a presbyter may pray certain prayers and administer the sacrament.[10]

- **'Lay' preaching with a prohibition against 'lay' administration distorts the relation of word and sacrament.** The welcome development of 'lay preaching' ministries over many years has raised the question for us in a pointed way. If non-presbyters are welcome to preach in the congregation but are prohibited from administering the Lord's Supper, then it is difficult not to conclude that the ministry of the sacrament is more important than the ministry of the word. Yet such a conclusion runs counter to the teaching of the New Testament (and compromises the balance of Anglican order reflected in *The Book of Common Prayer* and the Ordinal). There is no doctrinal reason why an authorised preacher of God's word should not be authorised to administer the Lord's Supper.[11]

- **Leading God's people as they gather to pray and hear God's word is always highly significant.** The role of administering the Lord's Supper should not be elevated above the role of leading the congregation of God's people gathers for prayer and the hearing of God's Word. Participation in the Lord's Supper is undoubtedly a significant part of congregational life which is genuinely beneficial. Yet God's people are not defined or constituted by this activity. Christians are disciples of Christ, those who hear and obey his word, those who love one another as they have been loved by God in Christ. Every gathering of God's people around God's word gives expression to this reality. While the specifics of each occasion may be different, one is not in principle more important than the other.[12] However, when a non-presbyter may lead the congregation at any time except at those times when the Lord's Supper is being shared, the opposite impression is strongly conveyed.

The nature of the Lord's Supper

- **The Lord's Supper is a proclamation of the gospel.** In the Lord's Supper Christ's people proclaim his death until his return. This is also done verbally in the preaching of the word of God. Since non-presbyters can preach the wonderful atonement of Christ in the congregation, what reason could there be for forbidding them from administering the Supper which proclaims that same gospel in another way?

- **A congregational activity.** The Lord's Supper is first and foremost a congregational activity rather than a priestly activity. The focus, according the New Testament, is not on what the person who administers the Supper does, or who he or she is, but on the corporate act of remembering the Lord's death through the total activity of thanksgiving, distributing and eating together.[13]

- **An authentic participation in the Lord's Supper does not depend on who administers it.** The current prohibition suggests that the validity of the Supper depends somehow on the person administering it, that a priest is needed to make the occasion authentic.[14] This is contrary to the theology of the Articles which insist that the efficacy of the sacrament depends only on 'Christ's institution and promise' and not the worthiness or qualifications of the minister (Article 26).

- **The Bible is silent about who administers.** The New Testament is silent on the identity of the person administering the Lord's Supper in the congregation. This is all the more remarkable since in 1 Corinthians 11 Paul was in fact dealing with disorder in the practice of the Lord's Supper.[15]

- **The word and the sacrament belong together.** It is important to note that while the important biblical and theological principle of not separating word and sacrament may have been expressed in the Ordinal by authorising the one person to perform both functions (and other persons to assist in both these functions in various ways), the same principle is also expressed liturgically in the order for the Lord's Supper in *The Book of Common Prayer*, where a sermon must be preached.[16]

- **The relationship of baptism and the Lord's Supper.** There is no sense in the New Testament that the sacrament of the Lord's Supper is more important or central than the sacrament of baptism, yet the contrary seems to be indicated by the fact that, unlike the Lord's Supper, baptism can be administered by a deacon or lay person.

Responding to theological objections

The discussion has been well served by those who have objections to the practice of lay administration, generously taking time to articulate the same. What follows is a brief summary of most of those objections and an indication of the response that has been made in each case.

- **A reasonable assumption.** While there is no New Testament evidence, 'it is a reasonable assumption that presbyters usually presided at church meetings, including at the Lord's Supper'.[17]

  Response: This objection concedes a major element of the argument for removing the prohibition (that Scripture is itself silent on the issue) and then makes an assumption on other grounds. Other contrary assumptions could be made in the face of Scripture's silence and in any case an assumption is not sufficient grounds for an absolute prohibition such as that which is currently practised.

- **The centrality of the eucharist demands an ordained person administer it.** Since the eucharist is central to the life of the church as the focal point of our unity with Christ and with one another, 'presiding at the eucharist therefore is properly exercised by the one who by ordination has been given authority and responsibility for the ministry of word and sacrament and who has committed himself wholeheartedly and permanently to this work'.[18]

> *Response:* The centrality of the sacrament in the life of the Christian congregation is questionable. It does not appear in this way in the pages of the New Testament (nor in *The Book of Common Prayer*, where sharing in the Lord's Supper might take place as infrequently as three times a year). Undoubtedly this activity of God's people is highly significant but that is not to say it is central. However, even if it were the most important thing that happens when Christians gather, it is not at all clear why this would demand an absolute prohibition on anyone but a presbyter from administering it.

- **The need to preserve the integrity of the eucharistic community.** It is necessary for the presbyter to preside when the bishop is not present in order to preserve the integrity of the local Eucharistic community.[19]

> *Response:* There are a number of points of confusion here: firstly, on the matter of what defines the community (i.e. the sacrament is not *the* defining reality of the church according to the New Testament nor even the 39 Articles); secondly, between the person who leads (or 'presides') on a particular liturgical occasion and the ongoing role of 'president of the community'. The presbyter has this wider responsibility, but this is not at all compromised by others administering the Lord's Supper in the congregation from time to time. Thirdly, there is no biblical or theological warrant for suggesting that episcopal ordination to the presbyterate is a symbol of the one, holy, catholic and apostolic church.[20]

- **No correspondence between leading at other 'services' and administering the Lord's Supper.** There is no 'binary correspond-ence' between 'presiding at Morning and Evening Prayer' and 'presiding at the Lord's Supper'.[21]

> *Response:* Every gathering of the congregation for prayer and hearing

of God's Word as a highly significant assembly of God's household. Those who direct the prayers of the congregation in response to God's mercy are exercising an important liturgical function. The one who administers the Lord's Supper is also involved in directing the prayers of the congregation in response to God's mercy. Despite substantial similarities, there are, of course, important formal differences between the two occasions. But there is no biblical or theological reason for suggesting that one is more important than the other.[22]

- **No necessary connection between preacher and the one who administers the Lord's Supper.** A reformed view of word and sacrament does not of necessity require that those licensed to preach should also preside at the Lord's Supper.[23]

  Response: The issue is not one of necessity but of removing an absolute prohibition. It is a matter of making lay administration of the Lord's Supper possible, not making it necessary.

- **This ministry is linked to pastoral oversight.** The proposed practice ignores the biblical principle of a conjunction between a ministry of Word and Sacrament and responsibilities of pastoral oversight.[24]

  Response: It is difficult to see where this principle is either annunciated or implied in the New Testament. The New Testament does not address the identity of the one who administers either baptism or the Lord's Supper in the congregation. Furthermore, this principle has never been part of Anglican practice. There has never been any question about an assistant presbyter, or even a visiting presbyter administering the Lord's Supper in the congregation. Their involvement has never been seen to compromise the pastoral oversight of the regular minister.[25]

- **The visiting celebrant is not strictly speaking an outsider to the church.** The visiting presbyter who administers the Lord's Supper in a congregation in the absence of a regular minister is an insider not an outsider because the basic unit of the Church is the Church of a particular geographically identifiable city, i.e. the diocese. The diocese is the local church or Eucharistic community.[26]

> *Response:* It is hard to reconcile the notion of the diocese as the local church with the New Testament terminology or concept of church. In the New Testament the word is almost always used of a group that actually gathers, i.e. a congregation (e.g. Rom. 16:5). Alongside this general pattern are a number of specific instances where reference is made to multiple churches in one geographic area (e.g. 1 Cor. 16:1, 19; 2 Cor. 8:1). The notion of a fellowship between congregations is certainly present, but the suggestion that the diocese is the basic unit of the church finds little support in Scripture. What is more, Article 19 defines the visible Church of Christ as 'a *congregation* of faithful men, in which the pure Word of God is preached, and the Sacraments be duly ministered according to Christ's ordinance in all those things that of necessity are requisite to the same'. The normal context of Christian ministry and fellowship is the congregation. The suggestion that someone unknown to the congregation and without any prior relationship to it is in fact a member is difficult to comprehend.[27]

• **Should we be speaking about every member ministry?** The New Testament does not in fact provide support for a 'ministry of all believers' but rather upholds an exclusive ministry of the word in the ordered life of the congregations. This means that the argument for widespread non-ordained ministry is based on a misunderstanding (though a more informal serving one another is clearly an expectation, e.g. Mark 10). Even Ephesians 4:11 need not be read in a way which provides support for 'every member ministry'.[28]

> *Response:* Ephesians 4:11 has quite regularly been read to say that the word gifts will naturally equip the rest of the congregation to be engaged in ministry as a result. Even though it can be debated as to what is the best reading of this verse,[29] this common reading certainly seems to catch something of the sense of 'every member ministry' that can be argued on other grounds. That the laity ought to be engaged in ministry both inside the congregation, as well as in

the wider community, could be argued from many different angles (for example, the principle of service; the list of instructions directed towards behaviour towards 'one another'; the household tables; the variety of gifts within the body of Christ; etc).

- **It would call into question the necessity of ordination.** The adoption of the practice of lay presidency would be inimical to the good order of the church, for if such a practice were to be approved the church would soon find itself with two ranks of presidents of the eucharist and this situation would call into question the very necessity of ordination itself.[30]

    Response: This objection rests upon a particular understanding of the essence of ordination, which places emphasis upon the sacramental activity of the elder or priest. It suggests that the authority by which the presbyter administers the sacrament is qualitatively different from that by which the non-presbyter would administer it. The language of rank exasercbates this problem. In summary, the understand of ordination assumed in this objection is difficult to support on biblical grounds.

- **A confusion between amateurs and professionals.** Authorising a lay person to preside would in effect be a quasi-ordination which confuses Anglican order and places well-intentioned amateurs in the place of properly equipped and trained professionals.[31]

    Response: There are a number of problems with such a characterisation of lay ministry. Once again, there is a confusion here about the nature of presbyteral ordination. Such ordination relates to oversight of the Christian congregation, not simply an authorisation to perform certain tasks.[32]

- **They ought to be ordained.** A layman thought fit by the bishop and congregation and willing to lead that congregation in this way ought to be ordained as a presbyter.[33]

    Response: If ordination is not merely granting authority to perform a specific function but recognising and granting responsibility to care for a Christian congregation, there may be host of reasons why this might be inappropriate in a particular case while that person's participation in this particular ministry of administering the Lord's Supper was entirely appropriate.

- **It would be preferable to restrict preaching.** Lay preaching itself is questionable as a development in keeping with good order. Following the precedent of Elizabeth I, there may be a need to regulate and restrict preaching rather than remove regulations and restrictions on the administration of the Lord's Supper.[34]

  Response: Lay ministry of the word is a welcome development which recognises gifts God has given to his church. These gifts are distributed to each believer 'for the common good'. There is not the slightest indication in Scripture that public teaching gifts are restricted to those who have been charged with pastoral oversight of the congregation. Lay people are licensed to preach on the basis of being tried and tested, including proven theological ability. The theological principle involved is more straightforward than any suggested historical precedent stemming from the reign of Elizabeth I, who, after all, had a range of political and other motives for acting as she did in regulating and restricting preaching.[35]

- **It is already possible for non-presbyters to be involved in 'extended communions'.** 'Extended communion', that is, the practice of lay people delivering the elements on the same day as the congregation receives them, under the supervision of the president of the eucharist is preferable to the proposed practice of lay administration.[36]

  Response: Lay ministry has its own integrity and is to be valued highly. It is not simply an extension of the presbyter's ministry and ought not to be restricted in this way. Furthermore, 'extended communion' is itself problematical. The practice of taking some of the bread and wine from one congregation (in which the presbyter administers them) to another (in which a non-presbyter does so) itself involves a departure from the practice envisaged in the Book of Common Prayer, where 'the Priest and such other of the

Communicants as he shall then call unto him, shall immediately after the Blessing, reverently eat and drink the same'. This practice was designed to avoid the kind of superstition that can all too readily attach to the practice of 'extended communion'.[37]

Conclusion

One of the earliest Australian recommendations on this issue, predating the Sydney Synod resolution of 1977, was based on a critical observation of congregational life:

> In most congregations, there is a natural leader, and consideration should be given (among other possibilities) to the licensing of such leaders to preside in that place for the ministry of Word and Sacrament.[38]

There are theological considerations even here, to do with the way God raises up leadership for his people during the last days. These have not been a significant feature in the debates to this point. However, the theological discussion to this point has provided sufficient ground for the Sydney Doctrine Commission, other assorted committees and the Sydney Synod itself to repeatedly affirm that 'there are no sound doctrinal objections to, and there are significant doctrinal reasons for, lay presidency at the Lord's Supper'.

ENDNOTES

1   *Lay Presidency at the Lord's Supper (1993)* §8.1, 469.

2   *16/94 Lay and Diaconal Administration of the Lord's Supper (1995)* §2.1–6, 427–8.

3   'A lay person is a member of the *laos,* the people (of God). In this sense an ordained person is a member of the laity,' Woodhouse, '"Lay Presidency": A reply', 5.

4   See Chapter 3 in the current volume.

5   Lightfoot, *Philippians*, 181.

6   *11/81 Towards a Theology of Ordination (1983)* §52, 374.

7   Chapman, 'Lay Presidency', 104–5. A similar point was made earlier in Lloyd, *Lay Presidency at the Eucharist?*, 29: '[…] the most striking thing about the evidence of the New Testament concerning presidency at the eucharist is that it is virtually non-existent'.

8   *Lay Presidency at the Lord's Supper (1993)* §2.2e, 463; Woodhouse, 'Lay Administration: A change', 8 in present text.

9   *Lay Presidency at the Lord's Supper (1993)* §4.1, 464.

10 *Lay Presidency at the Lord's Supper (1993)* §2.2d, 465.

11 Chapman, 'Lay Presidency', 106; *Lay Presidency at the Lord's Supper (1993)* §2.2a, pp. 461–2.

12 *Lay Presidency at the Lord's Supper (1993)* §2.2c, 462.

13 *11/81 Towards a Theology of Ordination (1983)* §37, 372. See also General Synod, *Towards a Theology of Ordination (1981)* §110, 44.

14 Woodhouse, 'Lay Administration: A change', 8 in present text.

15 *11/81 Towards a Theology of Ordination (1983)* §§37–38, 372. Even more pointedly: 'The New Testament is silent about whether there was a presidential role, let alone who filled it'; *Diaconal Presidency at the Lord's Supper (1993)* §2.6, 412.

16 *Lay Presidency at the Lord's Supper (1993)* §4.8, 466.

17 *11/81 Towards a Theology of Ordination (1983)* §46, 373.

18 General Synod, *Towards a Theology of Ordination (1981)* §105, 43; cf. Robinson, 'Lay Presidency: Another Point of View', 6.

19 Carnley, 'A Response', 3.

20 Woodhouse, '"Lay Presidency": A reply', 4, 2–3. *Lay and Diaconal Administration of the Lord's Supper (1998)*, 459.

21 Carnley, 'A Response', 3.

22 Woodhouse, '"Lay Presidency": A reply', 3.

23 Dissenting view in 'Report of the Synod Committee re 37/83 "Towards a Theology of Ordination": Lay Presidency at the Holy Communion' (1985) §6, 314.

24 Carnley, 'A Response', 5.

25 *Lay Presidency at the Lord's Supper (1993)* §4.5, 465; Woodhouse, '"Lay Presidency": A reply', 5.

26 Carnley, 'A Response', pp. 3–4; cf. Robinson, 'Lay Presidency: Another Point of View', 9, who argues every priest represents the bishop and so the visitor is 'equally representative of the local bishop as the rector'.

27 Woodhouse, '"Lay Presidency": A reply', 4.

28 Robinson, 'Ministry: Anglican Formularies and New Testament', 2–4.

29 O'Brien, *Ephesians*, 302–4.

30 General Synod, *Towards a Theology of Ordination (1981)* §107, 44.

31 Carnley, 'A Response', 5.

32 *Lay Presidency at the Lord's Supper (1993)* §4.5, 465; Woodhouse, '"Lay Presidency": A reply', 5.

33 General Synod, *Towards a Theology of Ordination (1981)*, 49.

34 Carnley, 'A Response', pp. 1–2.

35 Woodhouse, '"Lay Presidency": A reply', 2.

36 Carnley, 'A Response', 2.

37 Woodhouse, '"Lay Presidency": A reply', 2.

38 *Full Report*, 35.

3

Timeline: Towards Lay and Diaconal Administration in Sydney Diocese

Peter G. Bolt

In the Anglican Church change comes slowly, for decisions must be made only after appropriate consultation, discussion and public debate. The progress towards removing restrictions on appropriately qualified and authorised laity and deacons to be involved in the administration of the Lord's Supper has been discussed widely, publicly, and for more than a generation. These things have not been done in a corner, in isolation, and there has been no unilateral action.

The question of lay involvement in the administration of the Lord's Supper has emerged in various places for a long time, often under pressures associated with inadequate numbers of episcopally ordained clergy, and often in missionary or expansive situations.[1]

Traditionally, the *administration* of Holy Communion has been the priest's domain exclusively, but the deacon would *assist* him by handing out the elements, for example. In Australia, the discussion of lay involvement in the Lord's Supper began with the question whether lay persons might *assist* the priest in the administration, that is, whether they might become involved in the role traditionally reserved for the deacon. When it first discussed such lay assistance in 1968, Sydney Diocese found that its practice was already clearly behind that of elsewhere in Australia and the wider Anglican Communion.[2] The Report, presented in 1969, noted that the role of assisting the priest was traditionally given to the deacon, and that there was a legal consensus that 'lay persons are not permitted to assist in the administration of the Holy Communion, this office being reserved to "the minister", which term refers only to priests and deacons'.[3] Despite these impediments, however, it was acknowledged that 'the practice of lay assistance is widespread in other parts of the Anglican Communion', and the Committee had discovered that Bishops of 23 Australian dioceses permitted lay persons to assist in this way. Although acknowledging that if lay assistance became normal, then 'the relation of such a ministry to that of the deacon [...] would require consideration', the time had come to regularize this practice by a Canon of General Synod. By resolution 27/69, Synod recommended that permission given to suitable lay persons to assist in Holy Communion, and that the Archbishop-in-Council take steps to bring a regulatory Canon to General Synod.[4]

1969

Meanwhile, the discussion was opened up further, as to whether lay persons could do more than simply assist the priest, by actually administering the Holy Communion instead of him. Even though, more recently, the issue of 'Lay Presidency' has often been spoken of as if it is the peculiar domain of Sydney Diocese, the topic was actually broached under the auspices of General Synod. At the 'Conference on Mission and Ministry', convened at Canberra at the request of General Synod on August, 8–14, 1971, several issues emerged from the working groups, which could not be adequately resolved at this conference. The plenary session therefore recommended 'that urgent and adequate consideration be given to each of these matters, and to their implications, by the

1971

appropriate bodies of the Church of England in Australia'.[5] The first of these issues was listed as: 'Whether laymen might rightly be given a commission of local and temporary effect (i.e., not conferrring the ecumenical status and character of the ordained ministerial priesthood) to preside at and celebrate the Eucharist'.[6]

In 1973, when the General Synod *Lay Assistants at the Holy Communion Canon 1973* was promoted and passed, before being adopted in Sydney later the same year, it gave assent that, '1. Lay

1973   persons being communicant may be authorised by the bishop to assist the priest in the ministration and distribution of Holy Communion'. That this permission was unrestricted at this point is made clear by the second item assented to, namely, 2. 'The Synod of any diocese may by ordinance set further limitation to the doing of any act referred to by this Canon by any lay person'. The canon also acknowledged the right of the bishop to specify qualifications for the lay persons to be authorised under this canon.

The question of lay administration cannot be isolated from wider issues under discussion at the time. The burgeoning interest in every-member ministry and lay involvement—not to mention the ministry of women in particular—naturally raised questions about the nature and place of ordained ministry.[7] A committee appointed by Sydney Synod 1973, reported in 1974.[8] The 1974 Synod passed a flurry of resolutions in regard to 'a proper sharing of responsibility for parochial ministry', especially the involvement of the laity—including women.[9] When the committee set up to deal with these resolutions reported to the 1975 Synod, promoting the *Lay Assistants Ordinance 1975*, it was resolved that it required further consideration, and so it was deferred until the next year.[10] The Ordinance came before Synod the following year in revised form, along with a report on *Lay Ministry and Licensing*.[11] This report noted that, although the ministry of women had long been provided for by the *Women's Work in the Church Ordinance 1922*, and the *Order of Deaconesses Canon 1969*, there does not appear to be any legislation allowing or regulating a ministry of laymen in church except the *Lay Assistants Canon 1973*, which includes both men and women in its scope but does not extend beyond certain assistance in the service of Holy Communion.

In the midst of these various inquiries into lay ministry, the 1976 Synod also requested (12/76) the Archbishop to appoint a group to work on the meaning, value, and theology of ordination.[12]

At the August General Synod 1977, the Commission on Ministry, chaired by R.C. Kerle, Bishop of Armidale, tabled a report, which began with the premise 'Every Christian a minister', and spoke extensively of lay ministry within and beyond the Church.[13] At the same Synod, Peter Chiswell, later Kerle's successor, apparently raised the possibility of lay presidency, thereby becoming 'an early advocate'.[14]

1977

In Sydney, despite the General Synod Commission on Doctrine having declared that its members were not in favour of lay presidency at the eucharist,[15] Sydney Synod Resolution 9/77, *Licensing Lay Persons for Ministry of Word and Sacrament*, requested local discussion on the 1971 Mission and Ministry recommendation:[16]

> Whereas "the full report of the Conference on Mission and Ministry convened at Canberra at the request of the General Synod of the Church of England in Australia" 1971 referring to isolated congregations states "in most congregations there is a natural leader and consideration should be given (among other possibilities) to the licensing of such persons to preside in that place for the ministry of Word and Sacrament",[17] this Synod requests the Committee re Meaning, Value and Theology of Ordination to investigate the issue of licensing lay persons for the ministry of Word and Sacrament and to report to the next session of Synod.

After presenting Standing Committee with an interim report in 1977, the working group established in 1976 delivered its report to 1978 Synod, *Meaning, value and theology of Ordination*.[18] Synod requested

(10/78) that the reports be printed and circulated, considered by Standing Committee, and sent to the General Synod Commissions on Ministry and on Doctrine.[19] The Standing Committee suggested a review of the *Women's Work in the Church Ordinance 1922–1978* and the *Readers and Other Lay Assistants Ordinance 1976–1978*, published both reports in *Southern Cross*, and sent them to General Synod.[20]

When General Synod met in August, 1981, it appointed a commission to study lay ministry.[21] The General Synod Commission on Doctrine issued *Towards a Theology of Ordination*, with a section on 'Lay Presidency at the Eucharist' (Ch. 10), which noted the recommendation from the 1971 conference on Mission and Ministry to explore the licencing of lay people to preside in both Word and Sacrament. Instead of affirming such licensing, the Report concluded that 'a layman thought fit by the bishop and congregation and willing to lead that congregation in this way ought to be ordained'.[22] The Report showed no awareness of any complexity that may be involved in following such a recommendation.

When Sydney Synod 1981 met, it heard that the two reports from the *Meaning value and theology of Ordination* group had been printed and were available for sale, and that many of the recommendations were now being considered by the committee set up by 27/80,[23] concerning a bill for *Lay Persons Ordinance 1980*.[24] Resolution 3/81

1981

requested the Standing Committee to investigate how to implement the conclusions of *Meaning, value and theology of Ordination*.[25] The Standing Committee, in turn, asked the Legal Committee to advise on the necessary steps to implement three propositions from the conclusions through General Synod:[26]

> Ordination is primarily to a cure of souls: therefore only those in charge of parishes would be in priests' orders.
>
> It should be possible for women to be ordained as Deacons.
>
> It should be possible for Deacons to celebrate the Holy Communion.

To further the discussion on the General Synod Commission on Doctrine report, the 1981 Sydney Synod requested Standing Committee:[27]

> To appoint a working committee to report to Synod on the General Synod report "Towards a Theology of Ordination" and in particular to comment on: (a) the nature of ministerial priesthood; (b) the relationship between ordination and presidency at the Holy Communion; and (c) lay presidency at the Holy Communion.

The Standing Committee referred the matter on to the Diocesan Doctrine Commission, who had discussed it by Synod 1982, but requested more time.[28] Their 1983 Report disagreed with General Synod's *Towards a Theology of Ordination*.

> Since the [General Synod] Report, in our judgement, is in error regarding (a) 'the nature of ministerial priesthood', it can also be shown its conclusions are incorrect regarding (b) 'the relationship between ordination and presidency at the Holy Communion', (c) 'lay presidency at the Holy Communion', and (d) indelibility.[29]

The Doctrine Commission Report proceeded to examine the question of lay presidency, concluding that the word-ministry of the pastors and teachers equips other members of the congregation for their various ministries, and that 'presiding at the Eucharist is a proper expression' of the gifts of leadership that some members will have amongst the body.

The Synod resolved (37/83) that the Doctrine Commission continue to explore ordination, especially in relation to the concerns of Anglican theologians of the 16th and 17th centuries (part c), and that a committee be set up 'to explore the desirability and constitutional aspects of lay presidency at the Holy Communion' (part e).[30]

The work requested by the Doctrine Commission was tabled at Synod 1984 (*Synod Resolution 37/83 "Towards a Theology of Ordination"*), concluding that 'on the grounds of history and theology' it cannot be affirmed as 'an Anglican stance' to say that 'episcopal ordination is of the essence of a validly dispensed Sacrament'.[31]

In 1985, in order to catch up with the changing nature of the diaconate, General Synod passed the *Ordination Service for Deacons Canon 1985*, which was subsequently accepted by all Australian Dioceses. The service allows for some significant changes in the deacons' role, by permitting their assistance to extend to a complete administration of baptism, and possibly also of Holy Communion.[32]

When the Committee set up by 37/83 reported to the 1985 Synod, it affirmed 'the important principle that word and sacrament should be united'. It also stated that lay presidency is desirable in

1985 certain circumstances, insisting that 'a person should not be given authority to preside at the Lord's Supper unless he or she is authorised to preach and vice versa'. It recommended changes to the *Deaconesses, Readers and Other Lay Persons Ordinance 1981* to give effect to the proposal.[33]

In adopting these recommendations, Synod passed the resolution moved by R.H. Goodhew (18/85), that it 'endorses the principle of lay presidency and requests the Standing Committee to investigate ways the possible legal and other difficulties in enacting this principle could be overcome'.[34]

In response, the Standing Committee appointed a committee, which reported in 1986:[35]

> 3.1 the committee accepts that there exist no doctrinal objections to lay presidency in the context contemplated by Synod. This context includes the authorisation by the bishop of suitable and duly prepared persons in situations where the regular ministry in the local congregation of an episcopally ordained priest is not available. 3.2 The reason for stressing this context is that we see difficulties if lay presidency became the norm as there are some who would argue that it could alter the role of the priest whom they would see as a focus of leadership and unity.
>
> 3.6 We do not think that there would be a threat to the concept of the three orders if the Church allowed lay presidency as contemplated.[36]

3.10 The majority of the committee believes that lay presidency as contemplated does not contravene any 'principle of worship' of the *Book of Common Prayer* envisaged in Section 4 of the 1961 Constitution.

The structures of the Australian Anglican Church are very different from those of other provinces.[37] It can be described as being 'bottom-up', rather than 'top-down', since the real decision-making power is vested, not in the General Synod, but in diocesan Synods (where there is a large lay representation, also relatively unknown in other Provinces).[38] As well as protecting this structure, the 1961 Constitution also connects Synodical decisions at all levels to historic Anglicanism. Section 4 reads as follows:

This Church, being derived from the Church of England, retains and approves the doctrine and principles of the Church of England embodied in the Book of Common Prayer together with the Form and Manner of Making Ordaining and Consecrating of Bishops, Priests and Deacons and in the Articles of Religion sometimes called the Thirty-nine Articles but has plenary authority at its own discretion to make statements as to the faith ritual ceremonial or discipline of this Church and to order its forms of worship and rules of discipline and to alter or revise such statements, forms and rules, provided that all such statements, forms, rules or alteration or revision thereof are consistent with the Fundamental Declarations contained herein and are made as prescribed by this Constitution. Provided, and it is hereby further declared, that the above-named Book of Common Prayer, together with the Thirty-nine Articles, be regarded as the authorised standard of worship and doctrine in this Church, and no alteration in or permitted variations from the services or Articles therein contained shall contravene any principle of doctrine or worship laid down in such standard.

Provided further that until other order be taken by canon made in accordance with this Constitution, a bishop of a diocese may, at his discretion, permit such deviations from the existing order of service, not contravening any principle of doctrine or worship as aforesaid, as shall be submitted to him by the incumbent and churchwardens of a parish.

Provided also that no such request shall be preferred to the bishop of a diocese until the incumbent and a majority of the parishioners present and voting at a meeting of parishioners, duly convened for the purpose, shall signify assent to such proposed deviations. Such meeting shall be duly convened by writing, placed in a prominent position at each entrance to the church and by announcement at the morning and evening services, or at the service if only one, at least two Sundays before such meeting, stating the time and place of such meeting, and giving full particulars of the nature of the proposed deviation.

Given that the possible contravention of Section 4 of the Constitution was mooted, the Standing Committee asked the Legal Committee for an opinion, which was duly received by the 1987 Synod:[39]

There is no principle of worship involved, nor any principle of doctrine, in having a lay president [...] in situations where the rector (archdeacon or bishop) is obviously the president of the congregation, but the particular service, at the president's direction is carried out by a lay person.

A majority of the members [...] are of the view that there is no legal impediment to lay presidency [...] and that the view of the 1985 committee and the majority of the 1986 committee is correct in law.

A minority report was also submitted. Donald Robinson, Archbishop at the time, was not persuaded by the majority report, and he indicated that he would withhold his assent to any ordinance purporting to authorize lay presidency.

About this time the General Synod Commission on Doctrine also began to engage in its own discussion, after Peter Chiswell, Bishop of Armidale, had referred the matter,[40] requesting an update of the General Synod Reports of 1977 and 1981. The Canon Law Commission had also asked the Commission on Doctrine to specify which parts of the Holy Communion Service could only be said by a priest. In August, General Synod 1989 heard about both requests, but it was too early for any report to be made.[41]

Considering that Lay Administration had become an issue of controversy, the NSW Provincial Synod held early in 1989 requested that a working party be set up to examine Lay Presidency (Resolution 9/89). The working committee reported to the Standing Committee in November 1990, which then declined to refer the matter to General Synod.[42]

1989

In 1990, the General Synod Commission on Doctrine raised several objections to lay and diaconal administration, but Dr Peter Adam, a Melbourne member of the Commission, declared himself in favour, arguing that there were sufficient theological justifications for the Anglican Church of Australia to recognise Lay Presidency as Anglican. The Commission reported to General Synod, July 1992, that they had 'two prongs' to their inquiry: discussion of the doctrinal basis of various issues associated with lay presidency, and the itemisation of the case for and against.[43]

The General Synod of 1992 passed the *Canon Concerning Services 1992*, which recognized the need for variation within legally authorised forms of service. Although such variations were at the discretion of the minister, they were to be (S 5[3]) 'reverent and edifying' and not contrary to the 'doctrine of this Church'—with the provision that the bishop may decide any question in this regard (S 5[4]). According to Section 5(2), such variations could be determined at the level of the local congregation for occasions 'for which no provision is made':[44]

1992

> Subject to any regulation made from time to time by the Synod of a diocese, a minister of that diocese may on occasions for which no provision is made use forms of service considered suitable by the minister for those occasions.

The 1992 Sydney Synod referred two notices of motion to the Standing Committee, which were referred on to the Diocesan

Doctrine Commission for comment:

> In the light of Synod resolution 18/85 endorsing the principle of lay presidency and the further report to the 1987 Synod, Standing Committee is requested to bring to the next session of Synod legislation to enable lay persons to preside at the Lord's Supper.
> In the light of Synod resolution 18/85 endorsing the principle of lay presidency and the further report to the 1987 Synod, Standing Committee is requested to bring to the next session of Synod legislation to enable deacons to preside at the Lord's Supper.

In response, the Doctrine Commission produced two reports, tabled at the 1993 session of Synod, *Lay Presidency at the Lord's Supper* and *Diaconal Presidency at the Lord's Supper*.[45] Not only did each report find no theological objection to either form of presidency, *Lay Presidency* argued that there were 'no sound doctrinal objections to, and there are significant doctrinal reasons for, lay presidency at the Lord's Supper'.

In his 1993 Presidential Address,[46] Archbishop Goodhew expressed some reserve about Lay Administration. Despite the opinions of the Legal Committee and the Doctrine Commission, lay administration will raise general concerns for many. Although having no theological objections himself, the Archbishop was concerned about issues of order, the long-term effect on ordination, and the effect on relations between Sydney and other Dioceses. The Synod deferred the *Church Ministry (Holy Communion or Lord's Supper) Ordinance 1993*. In March 1994,[47] as well as deferring the 2nd reading of this Ordinance until the next regular meeting of Synod in October, the second sitting of Synod passed two resolutions:[48]

1993

16/93 Lay and diaconal presidency
This Synod notes the President's remarks in his Presidential address and requests the Archbishop to confer with the Standing Committee to investigate the impact of lay and diaconal presidency on church order and other matters relating thereto.

16/94 Lay and diaconal presidency

In the light of Synod resolution 18/85 endorsing the principle of lay presidency, the report to the 1987 Synod with reports that there existed no doctrinal objection and no legal impediment to lay presidency as contemplated by Synod, and the report to the 1993 Synod stating that there are no sound doctrinal objections to, and there are significant doctrinal reasons for, lay presidency at the Lord's Supper, this Synod requests Standing Committee, in consultation with the Archbishop concerning the matters raised in his Presidential Address, to bring to the next session of Synod legislation to enable deacons and lay persons, in appropriate circumstances, to preside at the Lord's Supper.

On 4th May 1994, Sydney Standing Committee appointed a sub-committee to consider the implications of these two motions and report back.

Also feeding into the 1994 discussion was a paper prepared at the end of the previous year (November 1993), by Archbishop Peter Carnley of Perth: 'A Response to "Lay Presidency at the Lord's Supper (A Report of the Diocesan Doctrine Commission of the Anglican Diocese of Sydney)"' for the General Synod Commission on Doctrine. In March 1994, Dr John Woodhouse submitted a reply to Archbishop Carnley's 'Response' for consideration by the Sydney Doctrine Commission. In May 1994, the Diocesan Doctrine Commission requested Donald Robinson to respond to both papers. Carnley had, in fact, voiced some criticisms, which Donald Robinson had himself raised. In June, Robinson submitted 'Lay Presidency at the Lord's Supper? Another Point of View', which urged Sydney Synod 'to think again', in view of potential breaches which may be caused 'both within the diocese and in relationship with other dioceses'.[49]

As part of the wider consultation desired by Archbishop Goodhew, the Australian Bishop's Conference 1994 unanimously adopted the report 'Ministry in Tomorrow's Church',[50] and the NSW Bishops were requested to bring a report to the April 1995

1994

Conference, with a view to making a report and recommendation to General Synod in July 1995. Appointed as 'special theologians', Drs Peter Jensen and Ivan Head assembled some reading matter, while Ivan Head also gathered together some personal responses from various people in the wider Australian Anglican Church. Archbishop Goodhew presented to the Synod in 1994 the statement of his own misgivings, previously shared with the Standing Committee.[51]

1995

In October 1994, the committee appointed by Standing Committee tabled their report: 16/94 *Lay and Diaconal Administration of the Lord's Supper*.[52] After articulating eight preliminary questions, the report discussed possible ways of proceeding, before outlining three possible models for lay and diaconal administration, recommending the third:

> Persons are permitted to administer the Lord's Supper who:
>
> (a) in the case of lay persons, have an authority to preach under the Deaconesses, Readers and other Lay Persons Ordinance 1981 and in accordance with its regulations, or, in the case of deacons, have a license to preach; and
>
> (b) have been approved by an appropriate Parish Council, churchwardens and incumbent and subsequently given an authority or license by the Archbishop.
>
> Such persons may administer the Lord's Supper
>
> (c) when invited to do so by the minister,
>
> (d) provided that the Parish Council and churchwardens have agreed to the introduction of lay or diaconal administration to the congregation in question.
>
> This model is narrow in terms of who may be authorised, but broad in terms of the circumstances in which a lay person or deacon may administer the Lord's Supper.

The report then canvassed three options for potential legislation: 1. The *Administration of Holy Communion Ordinance 1994*; 2. The *Ministry Ordinance 1994*; and 3. The recognition that no further legislation may be necessary, for the proposed model may be allowed under the *Lay*

Assistants at Holy Communion Canon 1973.

The second session of the 43rd Synod (which ended on 2 March 1995) passed the bill for *Preaching and Administration of Holy Communion by Lay Persons and Deacons Ordinance 1995* to the third reading stage. The matter was then held over until the October Synod.[53] This March sitting also requested (3/95) the Primate, under section 63(1) of the Constitution of the Anglican Church of Australia, to refer to the Appellate Tribunal for its opinion on the following question:[54]

> Would the Preaching and Administration of Holy Communion by Lay Persons and Deacons Ordinance 1995, if passed by the Synod of the Diocese of Sydney and assented to by the Archbishop of Sydney in the form now before the Synod, be consistent with the provisions of the Constitution of the Anglican Church of Australia?

A preliminary conference of the Appellate Tribunal was held on 2 August 1995, which granted an adjournment until after the October Synod.

Meanwhile, the question had also been occupying the attention of General Synod circles. At the end of the previous year, General Synod Commission on Doctrine had engaged in a consultation on Lay Presidency, which was published as *Lay Presidency at the Eucharist: A Theological Consultation.* Reporting to the 1995 General Synod, the Commission spoke of lay and diaconal administration being one of its major studies since 1992, and that the Sydney Doctrine Commission's two reports providing the focus for their 6th December 1994 consultation.[55] In July 1995, General Synod requested (Resolution 68/95) the Commission on Ministry and Training, and the Rural Ministry Task Group to bring to the 1998 session 'guidelines for provision of sacramental ministry to areas where stipendiary priestly ministry cannot be sustained'. The same resolution requested the Commission of Doctrine 'to contribute to the report an exploration of the indelibility of orders and of ecumenically shared eucharistic ministry'.[56] Pursuant to Resolution

68/95, the General Synod Commission on Doctrine held a second Consultation later that year, which was published in August 1996 as *Who May Celebrate? Boundaries of Anglican Order.*[57]

Also in 1995, the Melbourne Synod called for a report into Presidency at the Eucharist, and the Archbishop appointed a commission. After meeting six times, given the divergent views on the Commission, the commission decided to present two reports, one in favour and one against lay presidency at the Eucharist.[58]

1995

In October, the Sydney Synod received the Diocesan Doctrine Commission report, *Lay and Diaconal Administration of the Lord's Supper,*[59] which concluded:

> While the moves in Sydney towards allowing diaconal and lay administration of the Lord's Supper have stimulated wide debate over major theological and pastoral questions, the Doctrine Commission is not aware of major new arguments being advanced. [...] the majority of the Commission still considers the case for lay and diaconal administration of the Lord's Supper as presented in the 1993 and other reports is sound.

The Commission also printed a minority report from Donald Robinson, arguing that lay and diaconal administration was not consistent with the doctrine and principles of the Book of Common Prayer and the Articles.

Synod also received a report prepared on behalf of Standing Committee, which discussed the costs involved with the referral to the Appellate Tribunal and its possible outcomes.[60] In order for the Synod to discuss these issues adequately a motion was placed on the business paper seeking to withdraw the question of 3/95.[61] The 3rd reading of the bill was deferred to the first session of the 44th Synod. The withdrawal was requested of the Primate, who was willing for Sydney's reference to be withdrawn, but then referred his own questions:[62]

> [Question 1:] Is it consistent with the Constitution of the Anglican Church of Australia to permit or authorise, or otherwise make provision for

(a) deacons to preside at, administer or celebrate the Holy Communion; or

(b) lay persons to preside at, administer or celebrate the Holy Communion?

[Question 2:] If the whole or any part of the answer to Question 1 is YES, is it consistent with the Constitution of the Anglican Church of Australia for a diocesan Synod, otherwise than under and in accordance with a Canon of General Synod, to permit, authorise, or make provision as mentioned in Question 1?

At the request of 25 members of General Synod, the Primate also referred four other sets of questions, in regard to the legality of prayers for the dead, reservation of the elements, manual acts not allowed for by the BCP, and lay persons being involved in various parts of Divine Service.[63] A preliminary hearing was held on 14th June 1996, which called for written submissions to be made by 26 December 1996, and replies to them by 17 February 1997. The Sydney Standing Committee announced that, although it had decided not to make any submissions, it would reply to others as necessary. Given that the opinion from the Appellate Tribunal was pending, the third reading of the bill for *Preaching and Administration of Holy Communion by Lay Persons and Deacons Ordinance 1995* was referred to the next session of Synod.[64]

On 24th March, 1997, Sydney Standing Committee had requested its Legal Committee to provide a report for Synod on the Appellate Tribunal opinion and reasoning when it became available. However, by October, the 1997 Synod had to defer the 3rd reading again, pending the announcement of the Appellate Tribunal's opinion.[65]

In April 1997, the House of Bishops of the General Synod of the Church of England published *Eucharistic Presidency*, in response to a 1994 motion, which assumed that 'that lay presidency at the Eucharist is incompatible with Anglican tradition' before requesting an inquiry into the theology of the Eucharist and the roles of clergy and laity in it.[66] The bishops' report acknowledged that lay presidency had been discussed in Australia since the 1970s and in the Southern Cone in the 1980s, and that, although the Roman Catholic and Orthodox churches insist on administration of the Lord's Supper by the episcopally ordained, diaconal administration is permitted by the Moravian churches, and lay presidency (given pastoral necessity) by the Reformed and the Methodists (since 1946).[67] The bishops themselves favoured another option:

> In our own context, which is increasingly that of primary mission, the development of non-stipendiary priesthood in ministries of various kinds is proving to be a creative development. These ministries meet such arguments in favour of lay presidency as are based on the shortage of priests.[68]

1997

Meanwhile, in Sydney things had stalled. The October 1997 Synod heard that,

> the bill for the Ordinance 'was passed to the 3rd reading in 1995, but has been deferred each year since then waiting for the Appellate Tribunal's opinion on referrals about "lay presidency". The Appellate Tribunal's opinion has not yet been given although it is expected soon. In the circumstances, the Standing Committee recommends the 3rd reading of the bill be again deferred.[69]

On 11th January 1998, the Appellate Tribunal published its opinion on the Primate's questions and furnished reasons for these answers. To question 1 (a), the answer was 'Yes' (majority 4:3); to 1 (b), the answer was also 'Yes' (majority 4:3), but to question 2, the answer was a clear 'No' (majority 6:1).[70] The Standing Committee reported the Appellate Tribunal opinion to the 1998 Synod.[71]

> On 7 March 1996 the Primate referred 2 questions to the Appellate Tribunal about lay and diaconal administration of Holy Communion for an opinion under section 63 of the Constitution. The Appellate Tribunal gave its opinion on 24 December 1997.
> By a majority of 4-3 the Appellate Tribunal held that it was consistent with the Constitution of the Anglican Church of Australia to permit or authorise, or otherwise provide for deacons

and lay persons to administer the Holy Communion. However by a 6-1 majority, the Appellate Tribunal held that a diocesan synod does not have power, in the absence of an authorising General Synod canon, to permit, authorise or provide for diaconal or lay administration.

At General Synod in February, the Report of the Commission on Doctrine commended their two publications. While disagreeing with lay presidency, the Commission argued that ordination as a permanent vocation was not necessarily to the exclusion of other pursuits and so non-stipendiary priesthood need not be short-term. It also showed a great reluctance towards receiving the sacrament from other non-episcopal ministers and, while not favouring 'reserved sacrament' the majority were positive towards 'extended communion'.[72]

1998 was also a something of a turning point for global Anglicanism, and a turning point which would subsequently exert an influence on the lay administration issue. In mid-August, the Archbishop of Canterbury announced that Resolution 1.10 of Lambeth 1998,[73] passed by a huge majority, affirmed that 'this Conference, in view of the teaching of Scripture, upholds faithfulness in marriage between a man and a woman in lifelong union, and believes that abstinence is right for those who are not called to marriage'. A further pastoral letter from Canterbury in 2006, looking towards Lambeth 2008, noted that:

1998

> I do not hear much enthusiasm for revisiting in 2008 the last
> Lambeth Conference's resolution on this matter. In my judgement,
> we cannot properly or usefully reopen the discussion as if
> Resolution 1.10 of Lambeth 1998 did not continue to represent the
> general mind of the Communion.[74]

And, of course, the intervening years had been dominated by controversy, set in train by those who disagreed with Resolution 1.10, and were determined to act despite of it.

Returning to 1998, the continuing discussion on the orders of ministry was reflected in the Report into the Distinctive and

Permanent Diaconate, received by the 1998 Synod, which then requested (17/98) that:

> The Standing Committee prepare a report for the first session of the next Synod concerning ways in which the recommendations of the report, 'Concerning the Distinctive and Permanent Diaconate', 1987, have been and could be further implemented.[75]

Synod and Standing Committee had requested the Doctrine Commission to comment on (a) The 1997 statement by the English House of Bishops; (b) the reasons given by the members of the Appellate Tribunal for their opinions; and, (c) the submissions of the [Australian] House of Bishops and the Board of Assessors to the Appellate Tribunal.[76] After reviewing the views in the various items referred for their consideration, the Doctrine Commission produced its report, *Lay and diaconal administration of the Lord's Supper, 1998*.[77] It acknowledged that 'different views about lay and diaconal administration of the Lord's Supper often reflect and arise from different understandings of the priesthood, the Lord's Supper and the church' (§11). The Report concluded:

> while different understandings of these important matters have been highlighted by the debate, the Doctrine Commission [two out of ten dissenting] does not consider that sound theological arguments have come to light to overturn the main lines of the earlier reports of the Diocesan Doctrine Commission to the effect that a provision for lay and diaconal administration of the Lord's Supper is theologically acceptable. [...] The question of the desirability of this measure was not revisited by the Doctrine Commission.

The December sitting of the 44th Synod requested Standing Committee to prepare legislation enabling a five year experiment in lay and diaconal administration.

> In response to the Conference on Women's Ministry, this Synod requests that the Standing Committee bring to the 1st Session of the

45th Synod such legislation as would enable a 5 year
experimentation of lay and diaconal administration of the Lord's
Supper (in the presence or absence of the incumbent) as a principled
means by which we may reduce the tensions and synodical divisions
over the ordination of women to the priesthood.

Such legislation should provide for Standing Committee to
monitor and report to Synod on the operation of lay and diaconal
administration of the Lord's Supper at the conclusion of the trial.[78]

When it became time to debate the third reading of the *Preaching and
Administration of Holy Communion by Deacons and Lay Persons
Ordinance 1998*, a series of objections were raised on the basis of
Standing Orders, and eventually the motion was withdrawn for
another day.[79]

In October 1999, in what appeared to be a hard-won victory at last,
by a 346 to 194 majority, Sydney Synod voted to allow lay
administration of the Holy Communion for a five year trial period.
However, on 10th November, the Archbishop of Sydney issued a
statement indicating he had withheld his assent from the Synod's
decision, indicating that the Appellate Tribunal's opinion that a diocese
should not go ahead without a General Synod Canon weighed heavily
upon him. Archbishop Goodhew also explained that, since
Lambeth 1998, he had added his voice to the call for bishops 1999
not to act unilaterally in regard to homosexual issues, and he
felt that 'to act unilaterally myself and without wide consultation
would undermine my credibility in those ongoing debates'.[80]

Continuing the discussion on ministry, the Standing Committee
presented a report to the 1999 Synod in response to Resolution 17/98
regarding the permanent diaconate,[81] and passed resolution 21/99:
Priesthood and Congregational Oversight.[82]

Synod requests that the Standing Committee consider how the
practice of ordination to the presbyterate (priesthood) might more
clearly and consistently be linked with the "cure and charge of
souls" or congregational oversight'.

The time had also come when Standing Committee could further progress the lay administration issue:[83]

> By resolution 34/98, the Synod requested that we bring to the
> 1st session of the 45th Synod such legislation as would enable a
> 5 year experimentation of lay and diaconal administration of the
> Lord's Supper (in the presence or absence of the minister).
> A separate report is printed.[84]
>
> During the year, we received a report from our legal committee
> on the opinions of the Appellate Tribunal on lay and diaconal
> administration of holy communion.

Standing Committee recommended a five year sunset clause to be inserted into the bill presently before Synod. It also reported the opinion that the General Synod *Canon Concerning Services 1992*, adopted by General Synod in 1998, may permit a minister. to authorise lay and diaconal administration of Holy Communion, since this is an occasion 'for which no provision is made' (Clause 5(2)) under the authorised forms of service. Since a minister so doing would be unregulated by any Synodical decision, the report recommended passing some regulations for the practice of lay and diaconal administration of the Holy Communion. The suggested regulations gave authority to a vestry meeting of the church to approve such practices, and prohibited a minister from permitting lay or diaconal administration in the absence of such vestry approval. Notwithstanding the content of the rest of the report, the final paragraph noted that 'there is considerable doubt whether clause 5(2) of the Canon allows a minister to permit a lay person or deacon to administer at Holy Communion. Further, it is disputed that the Synod has power to make regulations other than by ordinance.'

Responding to concerns Archbishop Goodhew had expressed in his Presidential Address, the Synod also requested (32/99):[85]

that the Standing Committee:

appoint a committee to assess the potential impact of the

introduction of lay and diaconal administration of the Holy Communion in the Diocese upon our relationship with and standing within the Anglican Communion at large; and

report back to the next session of Synod.

The Synod of 2000 heard that, in response to Resolution 32/99, Standing Committee had appointed a committee to consider the matter, and when it reported in 2001, things had come to a stand-still:[86]

The committee has advised that it wrote many letters to people outside the Diocese seeking comment, but few responses were received. It is unlikely that this matter can be progressed much further at this time.

Despite the lack of response, however, the same Synod passed two Resolutions to continue the attempt to gain an outcome. Resolution 25/01 (Lay and diaconal administration of Holy Communion) kept the process going within the Diocese:[87]

Synod noting its own frequently expressed desire for lay and diaconal administration of holy communion and the Archbishop's comments that he wishes to find a constitutionally legal way to proceed, requests that the Standing Committee appoint a committee to investigate the options, if any, consistent with law, that are available and report back to the next ordinary session of the Synod together with any appropriate legislation.

The second resolution (26/01), sought to begin some movement at the General Synod, by urging Sydney's representatives to promulgate a bill for a canon to govern diaconal administration only:[88]

Synod requests that our representatives on General Synod, at the next session of the General Synod, promote a bill for a canon to permit a deacon to administer Holy Communion.

The following year, Synod 2002 heard that a committee had been appointed to deal with these two resolutions, but it had not reported, so both items remained outstanding.[89]

In 2002, those still chafing under the Lambeth 1998 Resolution 1.10, finally acted, beginning yet another turning point for global Anglicanism. Firstly, Michael Ingham, Bishop of New Westminster (Canada) authorised a service for blessing same-sex couples, and then, in the following year, on 5 August 2003, the Diocese of New Hampshire (USA) elected the openly homosexual Gene Robinson as its bishop.[90]

When Sydney Synod met in October, the report in response to 25/01 was tabled:[91]

> it is recommended that an ordinance be promoted to the next session of the Synod. Such an ordinance should repeal Section x of the Act of Uniformity in so far, if at all, it applies in the Diocese of Sydney. It should also ensure that no ordinance or any provision of any consensual compact in force in this diocese would prevent the archbishop from licensing a deacon or lay person to assist the minister of a church by administering the Lord's Supper in that church. The circumstances under which lay and diaconal administration should proceed at any service or on any church trust property could be dealt with by way of regulation of the Archbishop at the request of the Synod.

Although the Act of Uniformity was repealed in England in 1974, and in 1976 the Appellate Tribunal gave its opinion that it no longer applied in Australia, a local repeal was thought necessary in case it should prove a hindrance to Sydney's move towards lay administration, should this eventuate.[92] In the light of the Report, Standing Committee[93]

> Requested that the form of bill annexed to the report be redrafted and that the redrafted bill be promoted to the Synod at our request. An explanatory statement and the redrafted bill for the Act of Uniformity (Section 10) Repeal Ordinance 2003 are printed separately.

As a result, Synod passed Resolution 26/03:[94]

> Synod Requests the Standing Committee—
> (a) bring to the next session a bill which incorporates the recommendations of its sub-committee for consideration by the Synod at that session, and

(b) arrange for a formal debate on the bill at that session, and report to that session as to the possible consequences of the passing of an ordinance which authorises diaconal and lay administration and as to how any adverse consequences can be avoided.

In the following October, Synod 2004 was presented with the *Administration of Holy Communion by Deacons and Lay Persons Ordinance 2004*. As the issue had been discussed in Sydney Diocese across 2004, the debate became dominated by the question of what leadership the Diocese may or may not exercise on the world scene, and whether or not the lay administration decision may impede Sydney's influence on the more significant issues surrounding human sexuality. This became something of a powerful lever at General Synod, which met in Fremantle the month before Sydney's Synod. General Synod held small group discussions on the issue of Lay Presidency, and heard presentations from Peter Jensen, Archbishop of Sydney, and Dr Andrew McGowan, of Trinity College, Melbourne. As the discussion fed into action, 'a motion that sought to have the issues involved in lay presidency discussed at a local level was amended so that it became a resolution rejecting outright the possibility of lay presidency within the Australian Church'.[95] The wording of this rejecting motion was deliberately crafted in the exact terms of previous motions in regard to issues of human sexuality. Previously, the General Synod had declared that it 'does not condone' the liturgical blessing of same sex relationships (62/04), and it 'does not condone' the ordination of people in open committed same sex relationships (63/04), and now it declared that it 'does not condone' the practice of lay and diaconal administration/presidency at the eucharist in this Church (74/04).[96]

2004

In October, Sydney Synod passed a strongly worded resolution (14/04) that disavowed the suggested correlation:[97]

> Synod respectfully requests and strongly encourages the Archbishop, the bishops, other clergy and the laity of the Anglican Diocese of Sydney, whenever appropriate—to vigorously deny the view that

endorsing lay administration would be equivalent to the consecration of an active homosexual, and to clearly inform members of the Anglican Communion, both inside and outside of Australia that the Sydney Synod of the Anglican Church has on a number of occasions, by a clear majority of votes, expressed a view consistent with that view expressed in the Sydney Diocesan Doctrine Commission's statement of 1993, namely, that—"… there are no sound doctrinal objections to, and there are significant doctrinal reasons for, lay presidency (administration) at the Lord's Supper. There are also sound reasons based on our received Anglican order for allowing lay presidency (administration). In light of this the continued prohibition of lay presidency (administration) at the Lord's Supper does not seem justifiable theologically. Since church practice should conform to sound doctrine, practical problems related to the introduction of lay presidency (administration) ought to be dealt with, but should not constitute an obstacle to reform motivated by theological truth."

Synod also received a further report from the committee set up pursuant to 26/03, which had been reconvened.[98] It acknowledged the change in climate within the Anglican Communion as a result of the consecration of Gene Robinson and the severe conservative reaction, concluding that 'it may be prudent to delay the introduction of lay and diaconal administration'. Such a delay could not, however, be expected to diminish opposition, and:

In the judgment of the committee the only way to respond to such opposition is to endeavour to assist the other members of the Anglican Communion to understand the biblical principles underpinning the Sydney position.

In the meantime, since the Act of Uniformity Repeal Ordinance 2003 had not been activated:

Given the extended debate on this bill last synod, the committee considers it would be prudent to activate this ordinance, as a fulfilment of the wishes of the synod to prepare the ground for the authorisation of lay and diaconal administration, notwithstanding that the ordinance in and of itself does not authorise either lay or diaconal administration.

Following this recommendation, Standing Committee was also able to report to the same Synod, that the Archbishop-in-Council had set the date for the commencement of the repeal of the Act of Uniformity as 1 September 2004. However, with regard to the request for a bill to be brought:[99]

> We have considered the request in resolution 26/03 and have decided that, in the circumstances, it would not be appropriate to bring a bill to the Synod to authorise lay and diaconal administration. Instead we have decided to promote certain motions to Synod for its consideration. A report about these matters is printed separately.

This had implications for the proposed bill to General Synod:[100]

> In view of the report of the committee appointed to consider resolution 25/01, we do not propose taking any further action about resolution 26/01.

By Synod 2005, Standing Committee reported that they were still considering the motion.[101] The 2006 Synod received a report on 35/04 the use of the word "Priest", and heard of the Standing Committee's passing of the *Presbyter (Amendment of Terminology) Ordinance 2006*, and, with the Archbishop, amending the *Regulations re Authorities for Lay Ministry*.[102] Fact-finding about 'local priests' in other dioceses—a major alternative strategy to lay presidency in places of need—had also begun:

> We noted that, in relation to the administration of Holy Communion, many dioceses have adopted the practice of ordaining "local priests". We appointed a committee to enquire of other dioceses in Australia regarding the extent of the practice, the qualifications required, and the nature of this ministry.
> The committee is yet to finalise its enquiry and report back to us.[103]

But, alongside these various reports, the Standing Committee noted progress had slowed on lay and diaconal administration:

> Having considered the matter further, we appointed a committee to seek written expressions of opinion on the following question—
>
> What is the nature of any legal barrier(s) that would make unlawful the practice of a lay person or deacon administering the Lord's Supper in this Diocese?
>
> We asked the committee to prepare a report on the opinions received with a view to our making a recommendation to the Synod this year about this matter.
>
> The committee has not yet provided its report.[104]

Synod 2007 received the report from Standing Committee, *26/03 Lay and Diaconal Administration of Holy Communion Legal Impediments*,

2007

which finally reported on the potential legal barriers. Receiving differing opinions on the question, the committee noted that the differing legal opinions appeared to depend upon differing theological opinions, and that the way to test the legality may be through the secular courts. If it were to be assumed that the Appellate Tribunal's opinion was correct, the committee noted that there may already be General Synod legislation under which lay and diaconal administration would be permitted (i.e. *Ordination Service for Deacons Canon 1985*, the *Canon Concerning Services 1992*, and the *Lay Assistants at Holy Communion Canon 1973*), which meant that, 'for diaconal administration of the Lord's Supper, at least, there is a way forward by simply licensing deacons to the sacraments in accordance with their ordination responsibilities'. The committee therefore recommended to the Archbishop some adjustments to the licenses of deacons and suitable lay persons, and that a service for the Lord's Supper be prepared that did not require priests to say or do anything.

At the time of this present publication going to press (September 2008), it is expected that a motion will be on the agenda for the October 2008 Synod:

Synod

(a) accepts the report concerning legal barriers to lay and diaconal administration of the Lord's Supper which was submitted to the 3rd session of the 47th Synod; and

(b) affirms again its conviction that lay and diaconal administration of the Lord's Supper is consistent with the teaching of Scripture; and

(c) affirms that the Lord's Supper in this diocese may be administered by persons other than presbyters.

Conclusion

The progress towards lay and diaconal administration of the Lord's Supper has been slow and steady. At every step of the way, there has been deliberate and careful discussion, with wide consultation both within the diocese and beyond it. These things have not been done in a corner, and those from the wider Anglican Communion have also had time to comment upon the issue. The process of change is always a slow one within Anglicanism, but with such long and wide consultation and debate, Sydney Diocese cannot be charged with acting 'in isolation'—this is patently untrue. Given that the move towards lay and diaconal administration has been a long-standing conviction, the diocese has even been praised for its generosity in deliberately not following its convictions too soon—in contrast to those who provoked the homosexual controversies:

> The North American crises that began in 2002 can be contrasted with the lay presidency controversy in Australia, which did not escalate into an international crisis. In contrast to ECUSA and New Westminster, the Diocese of Sydney consulted widely and, despite a firm conviction that lay presidency was not prohibited by Scripture (a view it maintains), realised that it was not a matter on which difference of interpretation could be reasonably assumed, and that proceeding would have had consequences for the entire Communion and Sydney's place within it. Sensibly and properly, it did not pursue the matter unilaterally or in defiance of the Communion.[105]

However, given that the Anglican Communion is held together by bonds of fellowship, consultation never implies that a consensus must be reached before action is taken.[106] There is a time for listening, a time for consultation, a time for explanation, but finally, there must come a time for action.

ENDNOTES

1   See Chapter 5 in this volume.

2   Resolution 25/68, Lay Assistants in the Administration of Holy Communion, *Year Book 1969*, 281, requested a committee to report on the possibility of lay people regularly assisting the priest. Cf. Hilliard, 'Pluralism', 139: 'An early sign of change in several dioceses was the licensing of selected lay men and women as liturgical assistants to administer the chalice at holy communion'. Hilliard cites the liturgical changes in a few churches in the late 60s, such as St Philip's O'Connor (in Canberra) and Hobart and Perth cathedrals, which 'embodied the ideals of the liturgical movement' including 'lay people as readers and intercessors; the presentation of bread and wine at the offertory by members of the congregation'.

3   Report Re Resolution 25/1968: Lay Assistance in the Administration of Holy Communion, *Year Book 1970*, 442–443.

4   *Year Book 1970*, 348. See also Standing Committee Report 1970, *Year Book 1971*, 323.

5   *Full Report*, 31.

6   *Full Report*, 31. Item (iv) concerned whether women could be ordained to the priesthood.

7   Taylor, *Lay Presidency*, 6, identifies the Charismatic movement, in particular, as challenging 'latent assumptions that Christian ministry and the gifts of the Holy Spirit were restricted to the ordained clergy'.

8   25/73: Sharing of Responsibility for Parochial Ministry, *Year Book 1975*, 344–348; Cf. 18/73: Future Role of Diocesan Readers, 307–309.

9   6/74 Sharing of Responsibility for Parochial Ministry; 25/74 Future Role of Readers; 8/74 Vesture of Readers and Lay persons, *Year Book 1975*, 240, 245.

10   Resolution 25/75, *Year Book 1976*, 258.

11   See Standing Committee Report, *Year Book 1977*, 289; for the Report itself, see pp. 317–320.

12   Resolution 12/76, *Year Book 1977*, 244.

13   *Proceedings of the Fifth General Synod, 1977*, 335–344.

14   Hilliard, 'Pluralism', 144 n.58. He calls Chiswell, 'an early advocate of lay presidency'. The official proceedings show no sign of Chiswell's input.

15   *General Synod 1977: Reports* Vol. 3, 57–58; see also *Proceedings of the Fifth General Synod, 1977*, 278–282. By 1981, according to the General Synod *Towards a Theology of Ordination*, most of the Commission were still of that opinion (see pp. 43–45), although not all (see p. 44).

16   *Year Book 1978*, 242.

17   The quotation comes from *Full Report of the Conference on Mission and Ministry* (1971), 35.

18   The group issued an interim report in 1977; Standing Committee Report, *Year Book 1978*, 348–349; cf. Resolution 3/77, p.241.

19   *Year Book 1979*, 250.

20 Standing Committee Report, *Year Book 1980*, 300–301; see also 'Meaning, Value and Theology of Ordination', *Southern Cross* (February, 1979). Draft legislation was prepared, but it was still under consideration at 1981 Synod; see *Year Book 1981*, 271–272.

21 [Sydney] Standing Committee Report 1981, *Year Book 1982*, 299.

22 *Towards a Theology of Ordination* (1981), 49.

23 *Year Book 1981*, 242.

24 *Year Book 1982*, 303–304.

25 *Year Book 1982*, 251.

26 *Year Book 1983*, 296.

27 11/81: "*Towards a Theology of Ordination*", *Year Book 1982*, 254; cf. *Year Book 1983*, 302.

28 Resolution 17/82, *Year Book 1983*, 236, 359.

29 *Year Book 1984*, 372.

30 *Year Book 1984*, 238.

31 *Year Book 1985*, 459.

32 See Chapter 4 of the present volume for an argument to this effect.

33 *Year Book 1986*, 314–316.

34 *Year Book 1986*, 244.

35 Report of Standing Committee, *Year Book 1987*, 258–259. The Reports of the Synod Committee on Lay Presidency at the Holy Communion 1985 and 1986, as well as that from the Legal Committee, were published in *Year Book 1988*, 325–334.

36 It is interesting to notice that earlier fears of the deacon's role being threatened by having lay assistants at the Lord's Supper proved groundless as the practice became widespread.

37 For a brief explanation of its differences, see the General Synod website, http://www.anglican.org.au/index.cfm?SID=2&SSID=6. The Constitution is also available through this site.

38 In terms of raw numbers, Sydney Synod is dominated by the laity. Each parish is represented by rector plus 2 lay people. The archbishop can add clergy up to a cap of 10% (currently, about 24) and the standing committee can then match that number with lay appointments.

39 *Year Book 1988*, 330–334.

40 Chiswell to Commission on Doctrine, 23/5/1988.

41 *Reports to General Synod (8th)*, Vol. 1, Report from Commission on Doctrine, 50.

42 Report of the Lay Presidency Group to Standing Committee of Provincial Synod, November 1990.

43 *Report to General Synod (9th)*, Vol. 1, Report from Commission on Doctrine, 38–39.

44 http://www.anglican.org.au/docs/Canon%201998-13%20Services.pdf.

45 *Year Book 1994*, 459–469 and 409–422, respectively.

46 *Year Book 1994*, 300–324.

47 *Year Book 1995*, 267–283.

48 *Year Book 1994*, 345; and *Year Book 1995*, 271.

49 Carnley, 'A Response'; Woodhouse, 'A Reply'; Robinson, 'Ministry'.

50 *Year Book 1995*, 425–426. Archbishop Goodhew reported on the Bishop's conference on p.423.

51 '19/93 and Lay and Diaconal Presidency (12/8/94)', *Year Book 1995*, 421–425. See also 'The Archbishop's Statement', *Southern Cross* (December, 1999), 4.

52 *Year Book 1995*, 427–444.

53 *Year Book 1996*, 353, cf. 2/95 p.293 and 446–450.

54 *Year Book 1996*, 293–294.

55 *Tenth General Synod 1995*. Vol. 1: *Reports*, Commission on Doctrine, 10. Resolution 49/95 welcomed the report *Lay Presidency at the Eucharist*; see *Proceedings of the Tenth General Synod*, 43.

56 *Proceedings of the Tenth General Synod*, 48. Cf. Head, 'Introduction [1996]', 1–2.

57 Head, *Who May Celebrate?*

58 Melbourne Commission on Lay Presidency, *Presidency at the Eucharist*.

59 *Year Book 1996*, 422–430; conclusion is on p.428.

60 *Year Book 1996*, 446–450.

61 *Year Book 1996*, 446–450. See also summary in *Year Book 1997*, 474–475.

62 *Year Book 1997*, 474–475, which does not report on Question 2. This can be found in Anglican Church of Australia, *Appellate Tribunal Opinion* (1998), 1.

63 See *Year Book 1997*, 474–475. The Appellate Tribunal declined to give its opinion on these matters, see Report of Standing Committee to 1998 Synod, Item 5.4, *Year Book 1999*, 386.

64 Resolution 10/96, *Year Book 1997*, 363, cf. 368.

65 *Year Book 1998*, 350.

66 House of Bishops, *Eucharistic Presidency*, 1.

67 House of Bishops, *Eucharistic Presidency*, 9–11.

68 House of Bishops, *Eucharistic Presidency*, 61. In his book, *Voluntary Clergy*, High Church missionary Roland Allen argued for this option in 1930, and the Lambeth Conference of the same year conceded that in missionary settings such non-stipendiary clergy could administer the cup.

69 *Year Book 1998*, 350.

70 Anglican Church of Australia General Synod, *Appellate Tribunal Opinion. Reference concerning Diaconal and Lay Presidency (7 March 1996)*.

71 Report of Standing Committee to 1998 Synod, Item 5.3, *Year Book 1999*, 386.

72 *The Eleventh General Synod 1998. Book 4: Reports*. Commission on Doctrine, 9–10.

73 http://www.lambethconference.org/1998/news/acnspast.cfm.

74 Archbishop of Canterbury's Pastoral Letter, March 2006; For a report and the full text of the letter, see http://www.lambethconference.org/lc2008/news/news.cfm?mode=entry&entry=0EF2A684-EE2D-9FA2-F5CAA03F0133AE3E.

75 17/98: Distinctive and Permanent Diaconate, *Year Book 1999*, 367.

76 *Lay and Diaconal Administration of the Lord's Supper* (1998), *Year Book 1999*, 451.

77 *Lay and Diaconal Administration of the Lord's Supper* (1998), *Year Book 1999*, 449–459.

78 Resolution 34/98, *Year Book 1999*, 371. The conference on women's ministry was held on 16 May 1998; see the report in *Year Book 1999*, 473–475.

79 'Lay Administration Bill Founders on Standing Orders', *Australian Church Record* 1878 (1 Feb 1999), 9.

80 Archbishop Goodhew, 'The Archbishop's Statement' (1999). Cf. Year Book 2000, 402, which reports the bill as passed but not assented to.

81 See also *Year Book 2000*, 417 and 481–483 (the report).

82 *Year Book 2000*, 395. Since ordination is the Archbishop's prerogative, this resolution was referred to him; *Year Book 2001*, 463.

83 Standing Committee Report, *Year Book 2000*, 418.

84 34/98: Lay and Diaconal Administration of the Holy Communion, report for Standing

Committee, *Year Book 2000*, 490–492.

85 32/99: Matters Arising from the Presidential Address: Lay and Diaconal Administration of the Lord's Supper, *Year Book 2000*, 398.

86 *Year Book 2001*, 464; Cf. *Year Book 2002*, 435.

87 *Year Book 2002*, 404.

88 Resolution 26/01: General Synod—promotion of canon concerning administration of Holy Communion by deacons, *Year Book 2002*, 404.

89 Standing Committee Report 8.20, in regard to Resolutions 25/01 and 26/01, *Year Book 2003*, 443–4.

90 Frame, *Anglicans in Australia*, 188–189.

91 25/01: Lay and Diaconal Administration of the Lord's Supper, Report to Standing Committee, *Year Book 2004*, 392–401.

92 Frame, *Anglicans in Australia*, 186.

93 Standing Committee Report, 8:12, re 25/01 and 26/01, *Year Book 2004*, 370.

94 *Year Book 2004*, 340.

95 Frame, *Anglicans in Australia*, 187.

96 http://www.anglican.org.au/docs/Proceedings2004master.pdf.

97 Resolution 14/04: Lay Administration of the Lord's Supper: doctrinal issues, *Year Book 2005*, 402–403.

98 *Year Book 2005*, 456–458.

99 Standing Committee Report, 8.10: 25/01, 26/03 Lay and diaconal administration of Holy Communion, *Year Book 2005*, 438–439.

100 2004, SC report 8.11: 26/01 General Synod—Promotion of a canon concerning administration of Holy Communion by Deacons, *Year Book 2005*, 439.

101 Standing Committee Report 8.7, 26/03 Lay and diaconal administration of Holy Communion, *Year Book 2006*, 459–460.

102 *Year Book 2007*, 438, 556–558.

103 Standing Committee Report 7.7, Ordination of "local priests" in other dioceses, *Year Book 2007*, 433.

104 Standing Committee Report, 8.6, 26/03 Lay and diaconal administration of Holy Communion, *Year Book 2007*, 437.

105 Frame, *Anglicans in Australia*, 201. Bishop Frame regards Sydney's processes in the lay presidency debates as showing 'a capacity for generosity of spirit and a genuine regard for the divergent opinions of others within the Australian Church and the Anglican Communion', p.182; 'the diocese has shown genuine regard for prevailing sentiment within the Anglican Communion by recognising and respecting the limits of diversity that the Communion would appear ready to tolerate. Such regard, however, has been noticeably absent in other parts of the Communion in relation to another controversial issue, a matter on which the Bible is far from silent', p.188.

106 Cf. Rowan Williams' statement, 'Remember that learning is just that – not necessarily agreeing, but making sure that you have done all that is humanly possible in order to understand'; *Presidential Address, Lambeth 2008*.

4

The Authorisation of a Deacon to Administer the Holy Communion

GLENN N. DAVIES

Introduction

In 1996 the Appellate Tribunal of the Anglican Church of Australia was asked whether it was consistent with the Constitution of the Anglican Church of Australia for deacons or lay persons to administer the holy communion. The majority opinion of the Appellate Tribunal expressed the view that it was consistent with the Constitution for lay persons or deacons to administer the holy communion, as long as there was a canon of General Synod authorising such practice.

Without conceding that this opinion is correct legally or theologically, this chapter argues that following this opinion, it is legal for deacons to administer the holy communion within the Anglican Church of Australia, since there is a canon, the General Synod *Ordination Service for Deacons Canon 1985*, which authorises deacons to assist the priest by administering both sacraments.

The 1985 Ordination of Deacons Service

The *Ordination Service for Deacons Canon 1985* has since been adopted by every diocese in Australia. The new service was introduced on the basis of the changing shape of the diaconate and the perception that the 1978 service in *An Australian Prayer Book* was inadequate for setting out the responsibilities of a deacon at the end of the twentieth century. The 1985 canon, introduced into General Synod by the chair of the Liturgical Commission, was deemed an important step in revision of the ordinal, which came to full expression in the 1995 canon authorising *A Prayer Book for Australia*[1].

Two notable changes occur in the service. First, whereas deacons could only baptise infants in the absence of the priest,[2] the deacon may now baptise a candidate of any age and may do so, if appropriate, in the presence of the priest. Second, the authority to preach, which was previously dependent upon the bishop's explicit permission is replaced with the bishop's instruction: 'to preach the word of God in the place to which you are licensed'. In other words, the licence to preach, which was not inherent in the *BCP* service, is now constitutive of the order of deacon.[3]

Under the 1985 canon, both of these changes are highlighted in the words of the bishop when he gives the deacon a copy of the New Testament: 'Receive this sign of your authority to proclaim God's word and to assist in the administration of the sacraments'. These changes have been universally recognised as an authorisation of the deacon to preach God's word and to administer baptism to candidates of any age. This represented a liturgical catch-up, for many deacons had been baptising candidates other than infants, and there was already a general recognition that there are occasions when it is appropriate for a deacon to baptise, notwithstanding the presence of a priest. However, what is curious about the wording of the 1985 service is the explicit inclusion of the holy communion in the deacon's responsibilities. On three occasions the term 'administration' of the sacraments is used in the service, whereas the word 'baptism' does not occur at all.

From the bishop's instruction:

> You are to be faithful in prayer, and take your place with bishop, priest and people in public worship and at the administration of the sacraments.

In the bishop's questions:

> Will you take your part in reading the holy scriptures in the church, in teaching the doctrine of Christ, and in administering the sacraments?

In the bishop's authorisation:

> Receive this sign of your authority to proclaim God's word and to assist in the administration of his holy sacraments.

Clearly, the authority to assist the priest in the administration of the sacraments is an authority to assist in the administration of holy communion, as well as baptism. There is no differentiation in the service between the deacon's authority to administer either sacrament. In both cases the deacon is assisting the priest, whether it is in administering baptism or in administering holy communion.

Objections to Deacons' Administering Holy Communion

Three objections have been raised concerning the above interpretation that the administration of holy communion is included in the responsibilities of a deacon. First, the term 'administration' does not imply 'celebration' or the recital of the prayer of consecration. It merely means distribution of the consecrated elements. Second, the service only speaks of the deacon taking his or her 'part' in the administration, so that even if administration means 'celebration', the part of the deacon is to assist the priest (as is customary for diaconal ministry) not to take the place of the priest. Third, it was not the intention of the

General Synod to authorise deacons to administer the holy communion, because the law of the Anglican Church of Australia, as expressed in the 1662 Act of Uniformity, prohibits anyone other than an episcopally ordained priest to administer holy communion.

First Objection: Administration does not mean celebration (or consecration)

The use of the term 'administration' has had a particular reference in the history of Anglicanism to the conduct of the service of the Lord's Supper since the first English Prayer Book of 1549.[4] Moreover, the title of the service in the 1662 *Book of Common Prayer* bears the same wording as that of 1552 service: The Order for the Administration of the Lord's Supper or Holy Communion.

In Anglican formularies the use of the word 'celebration' is somewhat of a novelty, the historically preferred term is 'administration'. In Canon 71 of the 1604 Canons, there is a particular reference to the 'administration of the holy communion'.[5] In Canon 56, in reference to the duties of stipendiary Preachers and Lecturers, administration is equally applied to both sacraments:

> [they] shall likewise as often every year administer the Sacraments of Baptism, if there be any to be baptized, and of the Lord's Supper, in such manner and form, and with the observation of all such rites and ceremonies as are prescribed by *The Book of Common Prayer* in that behalf.

Richard Hooker refers to the term when discussing the objections of those who 'allow no invention of man to be mingled with the outward administration of sacraments'.[6] Similarly, in reference to the sacrament of the body and blood of Christ, Hooker states:

> they [the apostles] being the first that were commanded to receive from him, the first which were warranted by his promise that not only unto them at the present time but to whomsoever they and their successors after them did duly administer the same, these

mysteries should serve as conducts of life and conveyances of his body and blood unto them, was it possible they should hear that voice, 'take, eat, this is my body; drink ye all of this, this is my blood' [...][7]

By citing the words of Jesus, Hooker unmistakeably includes the prayer of consecration within the act of administration.

The language of administration continues to be used to this day in the Revised English Canons of 1969, where the heading of Section B is entitled: 'Divine Service and the Administration of the Sacraments'. The term is also specifically used of the Holy Communion (B12) and of Holy Baptism (B21). Moreover, the distinction is made between 'administer' and 'distribute' in these English canons.[8] Clearly the 'administration' includes the prayer of consecration and the service proper, while the distribution refers to that part of the service where the bread and wine are offered to communicants.

In the Form and Manner of the Making of Deacons (*BCP*), it is also clear that the administration of the Lord's Supper is not part of the duties of a deacon. The deacon assists, but it is the priest who administers the sacrament and the deacon also helps in the distribution of the consecrated elements.[9] It is not possible therefore, to reinterpret the language of 'administration' when referring to the sacraments as other than the conduct of the rite, whether it be baptism[10] or holy communion. This is the language of the Prayer Book and of the Canons of 1604, which continues to be used in the English Canons of 1969.

Second Objection: Deacons only take their part, not take the whole service

The language of 'assistance' or of deacons taking their part in the administration of the holy communion has been construed by some to indicate that the whole service is not in the hands of the deacon, this being the established custom of the Church of England. However, there is nothing in the canon to indicate this. Rather, the canon is undifferentiated in its description of the deacon's part in baptism and the deacon's part in holy communion.

It was the established custom of the Anglican Church to restrict deacons to baptising only infants, in accordance with the *BCP* Ordinal. Yet this restriction is plainly removed by the new canon. In other words there is a new part for the deacon to play. Significantly there is no other church law, other than the words of the Ordinal, that describes such a restriction.[11] Likewise, there is nothing in the new service, which prevents deacons from baptising a candidate in the presence of the priest. The absence of this *BCP* restriction is not accidental but deliberate, as it seeks to redefine the role of the deacon in baptism. This new role is still seen as assisting the priest, but such assistance may now be rendered in the presence as well as the absence of the priest. The concept of 'assistance' does not preclude the deacon's administering the rite of baptism in its entirety.

Since the canon is undifferentiated in its reference to the deacon's assistance in the administration of the sacraments—noting that neither baptism nor holy communion are explicitly mentioned in the canon—the expanded role of the diaconate may properly be seen in the deacon's assistance to the priest in holy communion as well as in baptism. The words of the canon are capable of being interpreted as a change in custom in the role of the deacon, superseding the role assigned to the deacon in the *BCP*. If the deacon is now authorised to assist the priest by administering baptism to adults, as well as infants, and in his presence, as well as his absence, then there is no justification for reading the canon as restricting the deacon's assistance to the priest by administering the holy communion in his absence (or even in his presence).

Moreover, the bishop instructs the deacon: 'take your place with bishop, priest and people in public worship and at the administration of the sacraments'. Clearly the deacon can take his or her 'place', exercising a liturgical role in the absence of the bishop. The deacon's activities are in relationship with the bishop and under his authority, but do not necessarily require his presence. Similarly, the deacon can exercise his or her role in assisting the priest when administering the sacraments in his absence. The deacon's designation as assistant to the priest does not prevent him or her from acting in the absence of the priest, any more than it prevents an assistant bishop acting in the absence of the archbishop. Mr Justice Handley makes a similar point in the following remarks.

> The role of the deacon, as defined in the Ordinal, is to assist the priest. If the priest was present at a communion service he (or she) would preside and the deacon would be relegated to the role of an assistant to the presiding priest. The situation would be otherwise if the priest was sick, on holidays, away from the parish on duty, or conducting services elsewhere. In such circumstances the deacon could 'assist' the priest in fulfilling his/her ministry to the parish by conducting communion services that the priest could not conduct personally
>
> [...] However the role of an assistant is not limited to situations in which the rector is absent.[12]

The language of the canon plainly authorises the deacon to assist the priest in the administration of both sacraments, not baptism alone. The canon provides no qualification of this assistance and no indication that the administration of either sacrament cannot be undertaken by the deacon.[13]

Third Objection: It was not the intention of the Canon to authorise diaconal administration

While the wording of the 1985 General Synod Canon may be capable of the interpretation offered above, it could still be argued that it was not the intention of the General Synod. Interestingly, a similar argument was proposed when the Appellate Tribunal was considering the constitutional change in the definition of canonical fitness for bishops. While it was argued that the change was not intended to allow for women bishops, the majority opinion of the Tribunal determined otherwise. In other words, they expressed the view that legislation is to be interpreted by the meaning of the words used and not on the basis of any supposed intention of the promoters of legislation.

In the words of Justice Keith Mason:

> The primary source of the presumed 'intention' of a legislative body is the language it uses. But to talk about a legislator's 'will' is largely fictional [...] Those who prepare or promote legislation (or any other formal instrument) have the opportunity to form it in their own terms, but they have no additional control over its interpretation. After all they are not the lawmakers.[14]

Conclusion

The Appellate Tribunal has expressed the opinion that the administration of the holy communion by deacons is consistent with the Constitution of the Anglican Church of Australia. However, for a change in the law of this Church to become effective, the Tribunal expressed the view that a canon of General Synod would be required to authorise such a practice. It is the contention of this paper that such a General Synod canon exists. The *Ordination Service for Deacons Canon 1985* expressly authorises the deacon to assist the priest in the administration of the sacraments. Such assistance equally applies to holy communion as it applies to baptism; and there is no dispute that a deacon can administer baptism in its entirety. It is therefore competent for the Archbishop of Sydney to license a deacon to assist the priest in the administration of holy communion as well as baptism, if the deacon has been ordained in accordance with the schedule of the 1985 Canon.

ENDNOTES

1   Significantly, when the 1995 Prayer Book was authorised by canon, the previous 1985 Ordination of Deacons Canon was not repealed but remained in force as church law. 'A Prayer Book for Australia' was not endorsed by the Diocese of Sydney, largely for theological reasons.

2 'It appertaineth to the office of a Deacon … in the absence of the priest to baptize infants.' *BCP* Ordinal.

3 The bishop's charge in the Ordinal of BCP states: 'Take thou authority to read the Gospel in the church of God, and to preach the same, if thou be thereto licensed by the Bishop himself.'

4 The titles of the first two English Prayer Books are: 'The Booke of the Common Prayer and Administration of the Sacraments, and Other Rites and Ceremonies of the Churche after the Use of the Churche of England' (1549); and 'The Booke of Common Prayer and Administration of the Sacraments, and Other Rites and Ceremonies in the Churche of England' (1552).

5 See also Canons 56, 57, 58.

6 *Ecclesiastical Polity* V.lxv.3.

7 *Ecclesiastical Polity* V.lxvii.4.

8 Canon B21.

9 'It appertaineth to the office of a Deacon, in the church where he shall be appointed to serve, to assist the priest in Divine Service, and specially when he [the priest] ministereth the holy Communion, and to help him in the distribution thereof, and to read holy Scriptures and Homilies in the Church', *BCP* Ordinal.

10 The title of the service in the *BCP* is 'The Ministration of Publick Baptism of Infants to be used in the Church'. However, the alternating use of the verb 'administer' and 'minister' in the opening rubric indicates that the two words were used synonymously.

11 The Ordinal, being a part of the *BCP*, was a schedule to the Act of Uniformity, 1662 (14 Car.2, c.4). Section 10 of that Act restricted the administration of the holy communion to episcopally ordained priests. See note 13 below.

12 Opinion of Handley JA in relation to the 1996 Reference to Lay and Diaconal Administration, 22.

13 Significantly there is no church law, other than Section 10 of the 1662 Act of Uniformity, which prohibits deacons from administering the Lord's Supper. Although this law has been repealed in the Diocese of Sydney (*Act of Uniformity (Section 10) Repeal Ordinance 2003*), according to the majority opinion of the Appellate Tribunal, diaconal administration would be lawful by virtue of a General Synod Canon authorising it, notwithstanding Section 10 of the Act.

14 Opinion of Mason P in relation to the 2005 Reference on Women Bishops, §§61, 64.

5

Lay and Diaconal Administration in Global Perspective: A Question about Sacraments, not Ministry

Peter G. Bolt

The Anglican Diocese of Sydney has been slowly and carefully discussing lay and diaconal administration of the Lord's Supper for almost forty years. Part of the strategy of those resisting this forward movement has been to declare Sydney's discussions 'idiosyncratic', 'unilateral', and the like, in order to isolate Sydney's proposals from the rest of the Anglican Communion in the present, and from the wealth of the Anglican heritage in the past.

On the contrary, Sydney is neither the first, nor the only, place in the Anglican Communion in which this discussion has occurred.[1] When considered from a 'global' perspective, in the geographical sense of the word, lay and diaconal administration has sparked interest from all corners of the earth. When considered from a 'global' perspective, in the historical sense, the present discussion continues a conversation about lay involvement in the sacraments, which stretches back through the period in which modern Anglicanism was being constructed, through the Reformation, and back to the early Church. When properly set within this global Anglican setting, it becomes improper to hijack the discussion into a debate about priesthood, for lay and diaconal administration of the Lord's Supper is a question about sacraments, not ministry.

1. Not just a Sydney Concern: A Global Issue

Although since the 1990s Sydney's discussion may have given impetus for a more focused and widespread discussion,[2] this diocese can neither take the credit for being the first, nor the only, place in which lay and diaconal administration has been suggested.

Lay administration is, of course, common in other Protestant Traditions, and Anglicanism has long-considered the dispensing of sacraments by dissenters to be lay administration. Within Anglican circles, what is officially endorsed for common practice must be distinguished from what may go on from time to time and place to place. Some have charged Sydney congregations with already practicing lay administration, although evidence is rarely cited to substantiate these inflammatory rumours.[3] On the other hand, the practice is reported even outside of Sydney. Even at the end of the nineteenth century, English evangelical Anglicans were receiving the communion from freechurchmen at the Keswick convention, although deeming it an extra-ecclesiastical activity.[4] In November 1902, in Arnhem Land, northernmost Australia, administration of the Lord's Supper by evangelical lay missionaries led to the closure of the Kaparlgoo mission, after a clash with the 'broadly tolerant' Tractarian, Gilbert White, first bishop of the newly formed Diocese of Carpentaria.[5] Although George Carey criticised lay administration when Archbishop of Canterbury, he spoke—with what Nicholas Taylor calls 'apparent unconcern' and 'retrospective prelatical nonchalance'[6]—about having practiced it himself as a young man in the airforce.[7] In 1981, the Australian General Synod publication *Towards a Theology of Ordination*, acknowledged that 'unofficially in some places congregations from episcopal traditions are celebrating the eucharist without a priest'.[8]

To move from practice to official proposals, lay administration was suggested almost a century ago—and not in Sydney. At the beginning of the twentieth century, Vedanayakam Samuel Azariah (1874–1945), Bishop of Dornekal in India (1912–45), suggested that lay people be authorised to preside at the Eucharist on occasion.[9] There were advocates of lay administration in England in the early 60s, notably Stibbs in 1961, and Beckwith in 1964.[10] In 1963 at the Anglican Congress in Toronto, a similar proposal was made by Canon Frank Synge, of Christchurch, New Zealand, and formerly of South Africa.[11] English evangelicals opened up the discussion further at Keele in 1967 and beyond, and the scene was 'if not seething, [...] at least looking for answers' by the time GS281 was presented to the General Synod in February 1976, where, for the first time ever, the matter was 'treated seriously in an official document of the Church of England'.[12] In 1977, a *Grove Liturgical Booklet* was published on the subject.[13] In the same year, the conference on Mission and Ministry set up by Australian General Synod urged a consideration of lay administration.[14] In 1984, Bishop David Leake of the Province of the Southern Cone initiated a wide discussion of lay administration, the Synod eventually deciding in 1986 not to act until further dialogue had occurred.[15] Diaconal administration has been authorised in Kenya since 1985.[16] In 1986, L. Boff urged a form of lay administration within the context of Roman Catholicism in Brazil.[17] The diocese of Armidale, in country NSW, discussed the issue in the late 80s and provoked a discussion at NSW Provincial Synod. Attempts were made to discuss the issue in English Synods prior to the 1990s, but it was stifled on the debating floor, and an attempt by South American bishops to place lay presidency on the agenda of Lambeth 1988 was similarly stifled by the section meetings.[18] In 1993, when 150 Anglicans from 29 nations met for 6 days as the first international consultation of the *Evangelical Fellowship in the Anglican Communion*, they heard that: 'faithfulness to the authority of Scripture and responsiveness to the pressing needs of mission and pastoral care, especially in parts of Africa, Asia, and Latin America, presses on us yet again the urgency of a theological evaluation of the merits of delegated presidency of the eucharist'.[19] In 1995 the diocese of Melbourne set up a commission to report on the issue. In 1997, the 10th Meeting of the Anglican Consultative Council spoke of a '"sacramental captivity", whereby gathered communities are deprived of sacramental worship unless a trained professional presbyter is available to them. [...] member Churches of the Communion should give urgent consideration to resolving that problem by studying the theological and practical issues raised by those who advocate lay presidency or "extended communion"'.[20] In 1999, REFORM (Ireland) joined the discussions on lay and diaconal administration,[21] and Nicholas Taylor speaks of advocates of lay administration amongst the 'fresh expressions' church planting initiative within the Church of England.[22] When Sydney Synod voted in favour of moving ahead on Lay Administration (only to be vetoed by her Archbishop), Bishop Elliot Sorge, former bishop of Sao Paulo, Brazil and Easton, Maryland, was amongst the first to congratulate the Synod's decision.[23] One of the most recent discussions (although beyond the boundaries of Anglicanism) has even arisen amongst the ranks of the Dominicans—after apparently first discussing the issue in the medieval period, even if only to dismiss it.[24] The issue has enough global interest that the time is ripe for a survey of the discussion, such as that of Nicholas Taylor, to be launched in 2009.[25]

The discussion of lay and diaconal administration of the Lord's Supper is by no means idiosyncratic to Sydney. It is already a global discussion.

2. Not destructive, but constructive: A Global Need

Proposals for lay and diaconal administration are positively motivated. There is no need to seek after sinister motivations, or to develop conspiracy theories about supposed destructive objects behind the proposals.[26] Wherever it has been suggested—and not just in Sydney—it has been with a constructive purpose, in order to answer, in part at least, chronic ministry needs arising from expanding gospel ministry and mission. Although solutions other than lay and diaconal administration have been suggested, it joins these solutions in addressing a global need.

a) A Chronic Emergency

A situation of necessity (or emergency) can be either acute, or chronic. The acute case of necessity has long been recognised in regard to the sacrament of baptism. In times or places in which infants frequently die in childbirth and baptism is regarded as essential—either for salvation or for parental peace of mind—baptism by a lay person (often a female) has been permitted by the Anglican formularies.[27]

Emergencies can, however, also be chronic. Contemporary environmental discussions, for example, have rightly drawn attention to the situation of emergency in which our planet exists, which has taken centuries to develop and will take centuries longer to be solved. If there is a situation of necessity to which lay administration of the Lord's Supper is a solution, then it can also be called a chronic emergency. In 1983, the Tiller Report recognised:

> the Church was not facing a temporary "emergency" during which bishops might authorise *ad hoc* arrangements, but a long-term shortage of priests and a need to made adequate and appropriate provision for the ministry of Word and Sacrament.[28]

In 1997, the House of Bishops published *Eucharistic Presidency*, thus recognising that Tiller's chronic emergency still existed more than a decade later.

Although a shortage of clergy can be an indication of a denomination in decline, it can also be a symptom of an expanding missionary situation. The supply of clergy to a vast territory has been a challenge in Australia from the beginning of white settlement in 1788. Early chaplains and Governors alike were concerned about this need, and as the population increased and spread out, the situation only grew worse. The correspondence of W.G. Broughton, Australia's first Bishop, indicates that the need for more clergy was probably his greatest concern.

Even in his first charge (1829), while still only Archdeacon, Broughton spoke of the many people in remote areas, the vast distances, and of too few churches:

> Seeing, then, that ordinary circumstances unavoidably deprive such numbers of our people of all participation in our public worship, and in one at least of the Holy Sacraments, how incumbent is it upon us to call to mind the solemn vow of our Ordination that we will "seek for Christ's sheep scattered abroad", [...].[29]

Broughton encouraged his clergy that 'much practical good' would come from them visiting their outer districts periodically, and 'by the celebration, which I should gladly sanction, of Divine Service, and administration of the Holy Communion, wherever a suitable station can be found, and a congregation can be induced to assemble'.[30] Evidently the 'chronic emergency' of this pioneering mission context allowed, amongst other things, the administration of the Lord's Supper in a place other than a consecrated building—something, strictly speaking, not permitted.

Broughton was by no means the first to face this chronic emergency, and his situation in growing Australia was simply the next arena in which an ancient battle was to be fought. With Taylor:

> The inability of Christian communities to celebrate the Eucharist for lack of a priest, is sufficiently ancient to have been addressed by the late second century Christian writer Tertullian.[31] In this sense it is nothing new, and it would little short of bucolic fantasy to suppose that every village in England was continuously served by a resident priest or priests from the seventh to the twentieth century.[32]

b) Proposed solutions to the Global need

One solution to this problem in the pre-Reformation era was Reservation of the sacrament, which has not been approved within Anglicanism since the Reformation, despite it being openly practiced in some quarters.[33] Faced with pressing needs for ministry and insufficient ordained men to supply it—with the sacrament particularly in mind—three different solutions have been proposed.

i. Non-stipendiary (or 'Voluntary') Clergy

In the early twentieth century, Roland Allen, High Church Anglican Missionary to China, sought a solution by breaking the connection between ordination and stipendiary ministry. In 1930, he set out his ideas in *Voluntary Clergy*, in time for the Lambeth Conference of that year to discuss them.[34] The idea met with a fairly cold reception, although not without some concessions:

> **Resolution 65: The Ministry of the Church – The Supply and Training of Men for Holy Orders**
> The Conference for reasons given in the Report of its Committee on the ministry cannot recommend a widespread adoption of the proposal that men of mature age and assured position might be called by authority, and, if willing, ordained to the priesthood without being required to give up their present occupation. But while declaring that ordination to the priesthood involves full and life-long service, not to be made subservient to any other interests, it sees no insuperable objection to the ordination, with provincial sanction and under proper safeguards, where the need is great, of such auxiliary priests.
> Further, in order to meet the present pressing need, the Conference would not question the action of any bishop who, with the sanction of the national, regional or provincial Church concerned, should authorise such licensed readers as he shall approve to administer the chalice at the request of the parish priest.

The final statement is an early concession towards lay assistance, in which lay persons are granted authority to take a role traditionally assigned to deacons. But this is not full-blown lay administration, which is explicitly rejected in a statement attached to Resolution 42. Here the provision for bishops to sanction exceptions to the general rule that Anglicans should receive Holy Communion only from ministers of their own Church, is declared to be *'not departing from the rule of our Church that the minister of the sacrament of Holy Communion should be a priest episcopally ordained'*.[35]

Although Allen was disappointed with these results, his ideas were later taken up with more vigour, and what was denied in 1930 as being improper to the calling of the priest, was actually embraced as time went on.[36]

ii. Extended Communion

An increasingly common solution to the chronic need for sacramental ministry is 'extended communion'. The 1981 Australian General Synod publication *Towards a Theology of Ordination*, describes this as when 'authorised lay ministers take the elements, consecrated by a priest in one congregation's act of worship, to another congregation'. In this second location, the lay minister reads the service of Holy Communion, omitting the absolution, the prayers of thanksgiving and consecration, and the blessing.[37] Opponents of this solution find little difference from the practice of reserving the sacrament forbidden by the Reformation formularies. Although this is put forward as experimentation with lay people presiding at the eucharist, the presidency still rests with the priest in the first congregation, and the lay minister simply 'extends' this ministry to elsewhere.

iii. Lay and Diaconal Administration

Lay and diaconal administration, as the third solution to the chronic emergency, takes the additional step of permitting a non-priest not just to deliver, but to properly administer the Lord's Supper.

Perhaps due to the constant and chronic shortage of clergy from the beginning, the laity of NSW have always taken a prominent role. The early Sydney bishops made good use of them, realising that, if they did not, people may not receive any ministry at all. Bishop Barker, Broughton's successor as Bishop of Sydney, for example, used the strategy of forming, in December 1875, the 'Association of Lay Readers'

> to afford help to the clergy by conducting services in the country and in small suburban churches or school rooms where the clergyman could only give a service once a month, or at most once a fortnight. By the aid of such laymen the services in such places were given every Sunday.[38]

As with the formation of a similar body in England, this was the first step towards having the laity actively involved in Anglican services.[39]

> Such men substituted for clergymen in conducting Sunday services, and were permitted to fulfil certain other ministrations in the absence of a clergyman. They were also licensed to preach. They were available where needed, though one imagines that a particular reader would probably minister regularly in the same place.[40]

This step, which was taken in many places besides Australia and England, began a trajectory that led inevitably to the discussion of lay administration. Thinking particularly of the early twentieth-century proposal of Azariah in India (already mentioned above), Taylor recognises the impetus of the global need when he states:

> it was precisely in a context of rapid church growth, with dioceses and missionary agencies unable to provide priests for young and scattered congregations, that the issue of authorising lay people to preside at the Eucharist was first raised in the Anglican Communion.[41]

3. Not a Global Crisis

a) The Current Crisis about Unity

Without doubt, the Anglican Communion is currently in a parlous state. Fears that it will become more fractured are certainly justified. It is therefore understandable that the rhetoric of 'unity' has become rather prominent. If unity is treated as the paramount virtue, then anything that threatens unity becomes the paramount vice. This, in turn, can lead to issues being lumped together, simply because they may threaten the Communion's unity, even if, when considered against criteria other than 'unity', the separate issues differ completely in kind.

b)Three Potential Threats

In this troubled Anglican Communion it has become fashionable to associate three issues together—namely, the ordination/consecration of women, the 'gay issues' (blessing of same-sex unions; ordination of practicing homosexuals), and lay and diaconal administration—as threats to global unity. A similar strategy was at work in *The Windsor Report*, when the Bishops reaching out to troubled congregations were treated as if this action was the same as the 'gay issues' that provoked the global crisis in the first place! Most recently at the level of the Communion, the three issues appeared together (with some other items) in this capacity in the Archbishop of Canterbury's *Second Presidential Address* to Lambeth 2008.[42] Within Australia, despite—or perhaps because of—more extensive discussion of the lay and diaconal administration issue, the linkage is commonly made.[43] This mistaken coupling of disparate issues—driven by fear of fractured unity—has so infected Anglican thinking that it has been one of the factors causing Sydney to slow down, to enable further conversations and explanations—especially with and to evangelical friends.

There are those, however, who have correctly noted that 'lay presidency is of a very different order' to the other two issues.[44] For constant critic of all things Sydney, Muriel Porter, the difference is found in lay administration not touching key human issues.[45] But this surprising claim negates the enormous energy behind the long press towards greater lay involvement in ministry,[46] and fails to account for why the issue has generated such heat in its opposition. Tom Frame, on the other hand, while also examining the three issues together,[47] concludes that lay presidency is *unlike* the controversies surrounding homosexuality, because of the manner in which it has been conducted:

> The North American crises that began in 2002 can be contrasted
> with the lay presidency controversy in Australia, which did not
> escalate into an international crisis. In contrast to ECUSA and New
> Westminster, the Diocese of Sydney consulted widely and, despite a
> firm conviction that lay presidency was not prohibited by Scripture
> (a view it maintains), realised that it was not a matter on which
> difference of interpretation could be reasonably assumed, and that
> proceeding would have had consequences for the entire Communion
> and Sydney's place within it. Sensibly and properly, it did not pursue
> the matter unilaterally or in defiance of the Communion.[48]

c) Fundamentally Different Issues

However, the three issues differ more fundamentally. Although each
is regarded as a threat to unity and each touch upon many aspects of
ecclesiastical and ordinary human life, and upon theological opinion,
the three issues are profoundly different in kind.

Firstly, lay and diaconal administration is not an issue of morality.
A wrong decision on this issue does not necessarily make someone a
sinner. On the other hand, the homosexual issue *is* a question of
morality, for—as has been recognized for centuries—the Scriptures
clearly list homosexual behaviour as a sin that is displeasing to God,
and which therefore attracts his wrath.

Secondly, lay and diaconal administration is not an issue of order.
The ordination of women was discussed as an issue of order, since it
was *directly* related to those who could properly be ordained to the
Christian ministry. Everyone recognises that the ordination of
women was an innovation, but some have accepted it as a necessity
of the contemporary world, whilst others have rejected it as a breach
of apostolic order.[49]

But it is important to realise that the lay and diaconal administration
discussion is *not* a question of order. To discuss the issue as if it is a sub-
set of priesthood immediately distorts the discussion.

This may sound surprising, since the issue is so often tied to issues of priesthood. This accounts for much of the heat of the opposition. When Primate of Australia, Archbishop Carnley helpfully pointed out that much of the present resistance to lay and diaconal administration of the Lord's Supper derives from a deep uncertainty about the nature and function of priesthood. Given the various changes and pressures that have stripped the priesthood of many of its traditional roles, lay and diaconal administration can be perceived as yet another threat to the priest.[50] But, as we will see below, the discussion of the sacraments as a function of priesthood is itself an innovation, dating to Tractarian influence in the mid-nineteenth century. We will also see that this innovation was resisted almost as soon as it arrived on Australian soil— and not just by evangelicals—by the High Church Bishop of Australia.

Lay and diaconal administration is not a question about order, it is a question about the sacraments. When it is discussed in the context of the sacraments, it becomes clear that the issue is the continuation of a long-standing debate regarding lay involvement in their administration.

4. Not Isolated from the Past: Lessons from Global History

Since the early centuries, there has been debate over the involvement of the laity in the administration of the sacraments. Although the present interest in the administration of the Lord's Supper may have only come to prominence in the last 100 or so years, it is, in fact, the next stage of this much older debate. Lay and diaconal administration of the Lord's Supper therefore finds its proper analogy in the centuries-long discussion over the rightness, or otherwise, of lay-baptism. Quite naturally, the most proximate context for discussing one sacrament is the other.

As we have seen, much of the heat in the discussion over lay involvement in the Lord's Supper has come from an apparent threat to the regular orders of ministry. When it was first proposed that the laity could assist the priest, the diaconate was felt to be under threat. Now that the suggestion has been made that the laity should be permitted to actually administer the Lord's Supper, the priesthood is said to be under attack.[51] But to connect this issue with Ministry already represents an escalation beyond its proper context. This escalation arose fairly recently, under the the mid-nineteenth century influence of the Tractarians. This can be illustrated from an early controversy within Australian Anglicanism.

a) Global lessons from mid-nineteenth century Australia

In the earliest period of the colony of New South Wales, ministry was supplied by hard-working chaplains, who were employed by the Government and loosely related to the Bishop of London, to whom foreign chaplains had been assigned since 1607 (the date of the founding of the first permanent settlement of English people in Virginia).[52] As part of the reorganisation which occurred in 1814, New South Wales became part of the newly formed Diocese of Calcutta, and, although no Bishop of Calcutta ever visited the colony himself, two of his Archdeacons, Thomas Hobbes Scott (1825–1829) and William Grant Broughton (1829–1836) successively served in New South Wales. Anglicanism in Australia was then further regularised in 1836, when Broughton became the first (and only) Bishop of Australia. In his episcopate the colony was subdivided into several dioceses, and other bishops were appointed.[53]

When the influence of the Oxford movement began to be felt in Australia in the 1840s, some of Broughton's clergy embraced the doctrine of Apostolic Succession with a new vigour. Broughton had no problem with this in itself, but they also drew the inference that those not baptised by episcopally-ordained ministers could not be buried in consecrated ground.[54] This real (and tragic) pastoral decision provides clear evidence that these men regarded such baptisms as completely invalid.

Bishop Broughton did not agree. In his 1841 Charge to the clergy of Australia, he did not open a dispute about the episcopate or priesthood, but, instead, he called them back to a proper understanding of the sacraments, drawing upon the tradition of the early fathers, as well as that of the great period in which Anglicanism was being formed.[55] As an old-school High Churchman, Broughton most certainly had a high view of the Church and of the Episcopate. He thoroughly agreed with the stress on Apostolic Succession, and he saw himself firmly within it. But he strongly disagreed with the inference being drawn from this teaching.

> By some it is maintained that the admission of [the Apostolic succession] involves a further consequence, that there can be no force or validity in any divine ordinance administered by mere laymen, or by such as do not partake of that successional appointment to the ministry. [...]
>
> The effect of this denial of validity to all ordinances, and to sacramental ordinances in particular, not being administered by lawful ministers, that is, in our sense, by clergyman episcopally ordained, has shewn itself in a refusal to inter in consecrated ground, according to the Order of the Church, such as have received the rite of baptism from lay hands, or those which are so reputed.[56]

Being greatly disturbed by this misguided inference, Broughton thought it right

> to refer to the subject, and to state my own belief that the refusal of interment upon such grounds is not accordant with a correct view of the nature of the ministerial office, or with the analogy of Scripture, and that it derives no sanction from the practice of the earlier Church, or from the ordinances of the Church of England.[57]

Although Broughton believed that the authority to minister and preach came from the imposition of hands, and this 'cannot be conferred by any other ordinary means or in any other regular way', he pointed out that 'it does not hence follow that God will withhold all effect from acts done by others not participating with us in such imparted authority', arguing the point from various scriptural examples.[58]

He also added a theological argument from the interconnection of word and sacrament:

If baptism at the hands of any other than a lawful minister be null, so as not to entitle those who receive it to Christian privileges, then also must the preaching of the Gospel by any other than a lawful minister be void of all spiritual effect; because the offices of preaching and baptizing are alike included in that commission of Christ to his Apostles from which our own is derived [Matt. 28:19]. Yet there are few probably prepared to affirm that the converting grace of God has in no instances accompanied his holy word when preached by those who followed not with us.[59]

In summarising the evidence from the early church and from Anglican divines (which he provided in two appendices), he noted that in the early church there were always those inclined to reject lay baptism as of no effect, but the judgment of the Church in general was against this view:

Indeed it must be admitted that authorities are not wanting which seem to lean almost to excess in the opposite direction; by acknowledging as valid and sufficient those baptisms which had been administered after an heretical form, by individuals under an actual sentence of heresy. [App. F]. The settled line of distinction however appears to have been this: that where the solemnly appointed form of Christian baptism was adhered to, the ordinance was admitted to be valid, even though administered by those who having no ministerial commission from the Church were regarded as laymen; but the heretics who baptized after any other than the appointed form were not recognized as giving Christian baptism.[60]

The Church of England has followed the practice of antiquity in forbearing to pronounce the services of a minister in holy orders essential to the validity of baptism [App. H].[61]

Broughton's arguments show that it is use of the correct form that was the key item, not the person who administered the sacrament. Speaking to the innovators of the mid-nineteenth century, Broughton reminded them of the Anglican tradition: it was not about the ministry, it was about the sacrament.

From his careful study of the relevant historical sources, Broughton was convinced that his Tractarian-influenced clergy had actually departed from their Anglican roots. He found the period of English history just prior to the 1662 *Book of Common Prayer* particularly instructive in this regard, for

> thousands and tens of thousands most piously devoted to the Church had failed to receive baptism at the hands of those whom alone they regarded as lawful ministers, not with their own free consent, not through any offence or fault of theirs, but solely through the cruel necessity of the times.[62]

Despite these numbers baptised at the hands of mere laymen, in 1661 the Convocation showed no inclination whatsoever to rectify the situation by seeking to bring 'lawful baptism of the multitudes who, during the continuance of the Great Rebellion had been excluded from it'.[63] There is simply no evidence that the validity of their baptism was even doubted, and, quite clearly, there was no form introduced to deal with the 'particular case of previous baptism by laics'.[64]

The long tradition upon which Broughton drew, was, of course, already enshrined in the Anglican Articles of Religion. The validity of a sacrament comes from the sacrament itself, or, to be more precise, from the the promise of God which it enshrines, and this is the true ground of its efficacy:

> Sacraments ordained of Christ be not only badges or tokens of Christian men's profession, but rather they be certain sure witnesses, and effectual signs of grace, and God's good will towards us, by the which he doth work invisibly in us, and doth not only quicken, but also strengthen and confirm our Faith in him. (Article XXV)

Since this is so, the efficacy of the sacrament does not depend upon the person who administers it, so much so, even an unworthy minister cannot hinder its effect (Article XXVI), or, as Broughton pointed out, a heretic.[65] To put it somewhat colloquially, the emphasis of the Articles is not upon the person who *delivers* the sacrament, but upon the person who *receives* it. The efficacy of the sacrament depends upon the promise of God it enshrines being received by faith (Articles XXVI). This is true of both sacraments, and it is certainly true of the Lord's Supper (Article XXVII, '… insomuch that to such as rightly, worthily, and with faith, receive the same …'). The significant thing is not *administration*, but right *reception*. It is not about ministry, but about the sacrament itself.

Three years later, Broughton made some further comments about the sacraments administered by dissenters—who were, of course, considered to be laymen. Because he had ordained two Presbyterian ministers, Broughton felt obliged to give some words of explanation in his 1844 Charge to the clergy. Despite this action, his high view of the episcopate had by no means diminished:

> the government of the Church by Bishops is the rule appointed by the direction of Christ himself, that through them alone can be derived a legitimate and sufficient authority to dispense the ordinances of the Gospel, and that peace and unity cannot, under any other appointment, be permanently maintained.[66]

And yet, at exactly the same time, Broughton just as clearly affirmed the validity of dissenting ministry—and dissenting sacraments. In fact, it was this affirmation that forced him to defend the two ordinations:

> The visible Church of the Redeemer is not limited to any one communion, whether episcopal or not; but embraces *all* who believe and are baptized after the ordinance of Christ. […] In the prayer for Christ's Church militant here in earth, "the Universal Church" is plainly described as synonymous with the term, "all they that do confess thy Holy Name;" and in interceding "more especially for the Catholic Church," we define it as consisting of "all who profess and call themselves Christians." It may be objected then, If you thus admit that all who believe and are baptized are already within the Church, and, in proportion to the faith of each, partake of the invisible graces of the sacraments at the hands of those who minister among them, what further object can be effected by the Episcopal ordination of the latter?[67]

In other words, according to Broughton's imaginary interlocutor, he ought to have no reason to re-ordain, because he is so certain than the sacraments—and we should note the plural—administered by these 'laymen' are already valid.

b. Lessons from sixteenth to nineteenth century England

The exposition from the Bishop of Australia is echoed over a century later by Roger Beckwith's foray into the same historical sources. After carefully reviewing the period when the Anglican formularies were being brought into shape, Beckwith identifies the great question as whether a layman might preach. Most divines (Cranmer, Whitgift, Thorndike, Forbes, Bramhall) recognised that a properly authorised layman might do this if the circumstances required it.[68] Lay baptism provoked a greater difference of opinion, although authorised by 1549, 1552 and 1559 prayer-books for emergencies, and approved by a range of divines (Cranmer, Whitgift, Hooker, Bancroft, Bilson, Thorndike, Sparrow).[69] During Elizabeth's reign, many Calvinist opponents of lay-baptism appeared (Rogers, Whitaker, Hampton Court Conference, Taylor, Forbes), whose opposition was 'often linked with a tendency to play down the general necessity of the sacraments to salvation'.[70] In the eighteenth century, the question of baptism by dissenters dominated the discussion. Since dissenters lacked episcopal ordination, this was regarded as lay-baptism. The debates continued into the nineteenth century,

> when it was ruled in a series of legal judgements that according to Anglican teaching lay-baptism in emergencies is both valid and proper. From that time opposition to the practice seems to have died away.[71]

Although 'almost all Anglican writers of the period when the formularies were being composed and brought to their present shape ignore the question of lay administration of the eucharist' (since it was probably not a pressing problem), Beckwith is certain that their opinions can be legitimately extrapolated from known attitudes to lay preaching and lay baptism:

> they regarded the ministry of the word and that of the two sacraments as closely bound up together, and were, generally speaking, entirely free from those sacerdotal conceptions which put the ministry of the eucharist in a class by itself.[72]

Some, for sure, denied that laymen may administer either sacrament in any circumstance (Rogers, Whitaker, Forbes, and the Puritan party),[73] but this was not from any sacerdotal opinions. They still considered both to be valid, but they objected to lay baptism and lay administration of the eucharist on the basis of Calvin's argument that 'the apostles simply represented the Christian ministry and not even secondarily the Church as a whole'.[74] It is important, however, to note that:

> the main stream of Anglican writers are unconvinced by this argument, since they reject it in the case of lay-baptism, and also in the case of lay-preaching (to which, by parity of reasoning, it applies equally). The obvious conclusion to draw is that, had they been faced with the theoretical question whether it is agreeable to the will of God for a deacon or layman, duly authorised, in case of necessity to administer the eucharist, they would here also have rejected Calvin's argument against it. And the only doubt remaining is, what they would have regarded as a case of necessity.[75]

c. Lessons from over 100 years of Colonial Necessity

As we have already noted, necessity may be acute or chronic, and the shortage of clergy and surplus of people needing ministry can be regarded as a chronic emergency. It is in the context of the needs of expanding gospel ministry that lay and diaconal administration was proposed in India at the beginning of the twentieth century, and in New South Wales at its end. Both of these former British colonies have suffered from the chronic emergency of gospel mission since the time gospel preachers first arrived in both vast lands.

The history of Anglican mission in India is particularly pertinent to the issue of lay administration. Even though the East India Company first went into India in 1614, bringing their own chaplains, Christian mission to India's indigenous peoples was not only not encouraged, but often actively discouraged, by the Company.[76] After the SPCK and SPG were founded (in 1698 and 1701), the Church of England increased in its missionary awareness, but the Company continued hostile to missionary efforts, ruling against them even as late as 1773.[77] The Societies were invited to support the Danish mission at Tranquebar, which had begun in 1709 with two missionaries from Halle, in Saxony.[78] In 1727, Benjamin Schultze, who had been at Tranquebar since 1719, also began a mission to the natives in the British dominions, and further centres of mission were gradually opened up.[79] What is significant for the present discussion is that the missionaries were all Lutheran.

These Lutheran missionaries administered the sacrament of baptism on a large scale. The Indian mission saw many converts to Christianity. By 1712, six years after the first missionaries had arrived, they reported 117 baptized Tamil converts and 35 Portugese, and that an additional work had begun in Madras.[80] 30 baptisms were recorded in 1717 and 50 in 1718.[81] Schultze baptized 200 converts in Madras.[82] By the high point of the Danish mission in 1740, 5600 converts had been made.[83] By 1776 even the least successful mission, Kiernander's at Calcutta, had baptised 495 converts.[84] In Tranquebar alone the number of native Christians grew from 3,700 in 1740 to 18000 by 1800.[85] The missionary Gericke in 1802 baptized 1300 people in Tinnevelly, and, in the course of a few months, eighteen new congregations were formed and 2700 persons baptized.[86] In 1814, when the first bishop, Thomas Fanshaw Middleton, arrived,

> he found an estimated 20 000 congregations in the Madras presidency. Amongst the Syrian Christian region, there were 88 Churches, 55 independent of Rome, with at least 13000 people under 144 clergy.[87]

All of these converts had been baptised by the Lutherans, but for the most part, under instruction from the Society, this was usually done using the form of the *Book of Common Prayer*.[88] The form was proper, even if the persons were irregular.

The Lutheran missionaries not only administered baptism (with the support of the SPCK), but, in what has been called 'one of [their] most interesting experiments',[89] they also ordained several native converts, according to the Lutheran rite. These men, in turn, went on to baptise a vast number of people converted under their ministry.

This is why these Lutheran missions are of such interest to Anglicans—and for the lay administration issue, 'for they are apparently an exception to the generally consistent witness of the Church of England to the necessity of episcopal ordination'.[90] The importance of the case study becomes even clearer when we realise that the missionaries did not act as mavericks, and it was not just the Society who supported their actions. They were also strongly supported and, indeed, praised by William Wake, Archbishop of Canterbury.[91] And—to get to the point for our purposes—the 28 non-episcopally ordained missionaries, and their non-episcopally ordained Indian 'local priests', also 'celebrated the Holy Communion according to the Anglican rite'.[92]

Understandably, questions were raised 'by anxious Anglicans',[93] from as early as 1713, and, by the end of the century, 'there was a strong feeling that the tradition of Episcopal ordination for both missionaries and Indian ministers ought to be restored and perpetuated'.[94] As CMS came to India from the beginning of the nineteenth century, for example, they deliberately assisted the Anglicanisation of the Indian ministry.[95] But in regard to the SPCK of the century before, the fact remains that

> an Anglican Society in the highest standing for considerably more than a century made use of the services of men, not one of whom, according to the strictest Anglican standards, was validly ordained.[96]

Now, there is no real question that everyone concerned in this century-long irregularity (including the missionaries themselves) were well aware that Anglicans regarded episcopal ordination as the normal and desirable practice. It is perfectly possible to argue that God in his grace was well able to work—and, in fact, did work—in the extraordinary circumstances of this time, without a proper episcopal ministry, even though episcopacy was nevertheless still of the very essence of the Church.[97] But this was not the argument used by those closer to the debate, as is clear in the example of Bishops Heber and Broughton.

d. Lessons from Heber and Broughton

Despite having a high view of episcopacy, both Heber and Broughton did not use arguments about *ministry*, but, instead, they argued from the nature of the *sacraments*.

i. Heber

The views of Reginald Heber, who succeeded Middleton in 1823,[98] are all the more remarkable given the fact that, in November 1825, he actually chose to re-ordain three Lutheran missionaries employed by CMS, and that he urged only episcopally-ordained ministers be sent in the future.[99] He had argued earlier (in 1812), when answering those who desired to rebaptise persons baptised by non-episcopal ministers, that:

> The German Lutheran clergy are as absolutely without episcopal ordination, and therefore in the view of an episcopal church as merely laymen, as the dissenting teachers in our own country. Yet [...] who has blamed the venerable Societies for the Propagation of the Gospel and for Promoting Christian Knowledge for recognising not only the baptism but the ordination of Lutheran Superintendents and Elders, and employing as missionaries those who, if your correspondent were correct, are not entitled to receive the Eucharist themselves?[100]

Later, when defending his re-ordinations, although he strongly denied that he admitted as valid 'ordination by Presbyters without a Bishop', he was just as certain that 'those good men are not to be censured who perpetuate [the needful continuance of ministers] by the best means in their power', and he would have no qualms about receiving the 'preaching and Sacramental ordinances of the Lutheran evangelical church, not doubting that they are a true Church of Christ, and that the Spirit of God is with them as, I trust, he is with us also'.[101]

ii. Broughton

We have already noticed that, when facing the same issue in the Australian context, Bishop Broughton argued from the nature of the sacraments. It is also important to remember that, in this earlier period, since Australia began as part of the Diocese of Calcutta, Indian Anglican history is, in a sense, part of the history of Anglicanism in New South Wales. Despite the fact that Archdeacons Scott and Broughton both had almost episcopal authority in practice,[102] they were nevertheless under the jurisdiction of Calcutta.

By this stage, increasing dissatisfaction with the Indian situation had arisen, and it is no surprise that Broughton, too, viewed it with some discomfort—especially in the face of the pressing needs for ministry in the expanding colonial situation:

> if you will look over the history of the Missionary attempts of the SPCK in India, you will at once perceive the difficulties and unsatisfactory expedients which they were reduced to; and if it be a subject of deep regret that no systematic plan was devised for the removal of those wants, which were felt at so early a period, how much more must we acknowledge the necessity of it now, when the whole world is besieging the Church of England with demands for Clergymen, qualified to carry forth into all lands the sound of those truths, of which it is her glory to be the appointed guardian.[103]

Given his full knowledge of the situation that prevailed in 'his' diocese for over a century, Broughton's approach is all the more interesting. As he writes here to his friend Edward Coleridge, he is anxious to prevent a similar situation in Australia, and the way to prevent it is to send more clergymen to diminish the need for such emergency measures. He does not, in fact, enter into a discussion about validity at all, but speaks of the massive needs that 'reduced them' to it.

Broughton also had personal experience of the need for emergency measures. In his visitation of Van Diemen's Land, Broughton had conducted confirmations, despite him still being an Archdeacon at that time. His freedom in this matter is instructive. Broughton did not conduct the confirmations on his own authority, but he 'had the authority of his diocesan, Bishop Daniel Wilson, of Calcutta, to admit to Holy Communion those who were ready and desirous to be confirmed, and exercised this right during his stay in Tasmania'.[104] Acting upon such delegated authority is consistent with his High Church principles, in which the Bishop was the one who had responsibility for ministry in a diocese, and any ministry undertaken by the clergy in his diocese is, in fact, delegated to them from their Bishop. This argument can be traced back to Tertullian, who expressed this view in the context of the administration of baptism:

> The chief priest, that is the Bishop, holds authority to baptise; and derivatively the Priests and Deacons; but not without the sanction of the Bishop, on account of the subordination of the Church, which being maintained peace is secure. (*On Baptism*, 17)[105]

This view of the bishop brings us to a further observation in regard to the present discussion.

e. Lessons from the High Churchmen

Neither the SPCK or Heber in India, nor Broughton in Australia, were representatives of the evangelical arm of Anglicanism. They were, in fact, representatives of the old High Church party, and each had their own clashes with evangelicals. Their view of the efficacy of the sacrament, protected as it was through its administration in the appropriate form, enabled them to accept as valid sacraments administered by dissenters—that is, by laymen.

But even if the High Churchmen discussed the issue in relation to the ministry, they would be able to do so without feeling like the priesthood was under threat at all. To illustrate from a more recent example, well before Sydney began its discussion, Canon Frank Synge in 1963, Principal of Christchurch Theological College in New Zealand and formerly of St Paul's Theological College in Grahamstown, South Africa,[106] argued that lay administration was a completely legitimate solution to the globally recognised need for sacramental ministry. To do so, Synge drew upon the same High Church view of the episcopacy as Broughton and Heber a century before him. At the same time, he delivered a strong critique of an over-inflated view of the priesthood that had had disastrous consequences for the Church:

> May I in one devastating sentence summarize what I conceive to be one cause of failure of the Anglican Church to answer its vocation to be the People of God? The clergy have entrenched themselves in the area of oversight or *episcope* as though they had the right to be there, thus converting a twofold tool of Christ, episcopate and laity, into a twofold institution, laity and clergy; the laity's vocation now becomes the support of the clergy and the vocation of the episcopate becomes the oversight by a senior clergyman of clerical machinery.[107]

Synge argued that there were only two orders of ministry, Bishop and laity, and—with echoes of Broughton's 'imparted authority'[108]—the bishop delegated his authority 'first to presbyters and then in emergencies to anyone'.[109] He questioned whether the Bishop delegates 'the right to eucharistize' because there is something about this that is inherent to the priesthood. He argues against the common solution of 'part-time priests' (i.e., Allen's 'voluntary clergy') because it is a solution that derives from 'a presbyterate that insists that the right of eucharistizing inheres in the presbyterate. [...] in order to have a valid Eucharist, so runs the doctrine, it is necessary to have a priest'. This rests on

> an insufficiently high doctrine of the Church and an insufficiently high doctrine of episcopacy and an unwarrantably high doctrine of the presbyterate. A high doctrine of the Church maintains that

Christ's ministry to the world is committed to the Church and that his oversight of the Church is committed to the overseer, the bishop.[110]

Once upon a time the bishop delegated his eucharistizing to laymen. It is true that they were called presbyters, but that title indicated that they were responsible and mature men; it did not indicate that they were not laymen. The bishop did it once when numbers and distances and disturbed times required it. Let him do it again. He did it once, not as a temporary and makeshift expedient, but out of a high doctrine of the Church; he did it because to him had been committed Christ's ministry to the Church. A Christological urgency and not merely an administrative urgency moved the bishop to delegate. That same urgency presses upon him today.[111]

The layman to whom the bishop would thus delegate his power to eucharistize would remain a layman. He would remain a layman unless the bishop decides, or until the bishop decides, that he is to be given lifelong delegation.[112]

A high doctrine of the Church prevents this proposal collapsing into congregationalism, and a high view of the episcopate says that the eucharist is that of the whole church and so only the bishop has the right to appoint a 'eucharistizer'. The eucharist is not the main task of the priest, but

the preaching, teaching, and directing are the presbyter's main task. Therefore the presbyter must be well trained; and the fewer presbyters there are, the more imperative it becomes that the standard of training is high.[113]

Whether or not all the elements of this argument will convince people today more than they did in 1963, Synge's argument is noteworthy in that it shows how lay administration can not only be forgiven in an emergency situation (as with Broughton and Heber), but can actually be accommodated into a high view of the church and the episcopate, and in a way that gives an immensely important role to the presbyter, while at the same time removing the eucharist from the centre of priesthood. In other words, even if the question of lay administration were to be approached from the perspective of the ministry (rather than the sacraments), then it is possible to do this in a way that does not threaten Anglican order at all.

5. The balance of the Sydney proposals

This brings us back to the Sydney proposals, for, in fact, these kinds of arguments are not simply those of the High Churchmen, they can be propounded as those of the Anglican formularies.

With almost forty years of scrutiny, both from insiders and outsiders, Sydney's proposals for lay and diaconal administration of the Lord's Supper have become rather finely balanced. Both friends and opponents recognise the strong evangelical heritage and ethos within Sydney Diocese.[114] However, even a fair-minded critic ought to realise that within its prevailing evangelical environment, Sydney Diocese contains a variety of opinion, and this is what ensures that most issues are debated fairly vigorously. In such an environment, the synodical process moves slowly, and alternative viewpoints manage to make their own impact upon the shape of the decisions that eventuate.

One important example of this phenomenon is Donald Robinson, who has played a prominent part in the discussions across the course of the long debate. Whereas Sydney's renowned 'congregational' tendencies may reflect the view of the ministry which, according to Archbishop Carnley, makes the clergy differ from the laity only 'by degree', rather than 'by kind',[115] Robinson's view of the bishop stands firmly in the trajectory that ran from Tertullian through Heber and Broughton: 'in our system, all priests are the surrogates of the bishop of the diocese'.[116] Sydney's mix of views on the relation of laity and clergy, both 'from below' and 'from above', has influenced the kind of 'controls' that are built in to the lay and diaconal administration proposals.

For it is only serious misunderstanding, at best, or scurrilous political tactics, at worse, to imply or assert that proposals for lay administration amount to a completely anarchic system, in which every lay person 'does what is right in their own eyes'. This kind of propaganda is far more inflammatory than the issue itself needs to be.

More sober assessments have recognised that Sydney's proposals have always included appropriate checks and balances,[117] and they come from both directions. From below, from above. A congregational meeting must agree to the introduction of lay administration. The bishop must licence the suitably qualified lay persons who are selected to assist the presbyter in this way. The lay persons are never operating in their own right, but their authority to administer the Lord's Supper is delegated authority: from the bishop, to assist the presbyter, recognised by the congregation.

It was the kind of protections built into Sydney's proposals, that gave grounds for the opinion of the General Synod's Appellate Tribunal that lay and diaconal administration of the Lord's Supper, as proposed, was consistent with the 1961 Constitution of the Anglican Church of Australia.[118] Because the presbyter never loses the oversight of the congregation, then the fact that a suitably qualified and licensed lay person may be delegated to preach, or to baptise, or to administer the Lord's Supper, never threatens the priesthood. In fact, as the Bishop of Bathurst put it:

> the priest's oversight is not undermined but exercised. Delegation of presidency [of the eucharist] *per se* does not undermine the distinctiveness of the order priest/presbyter and therefore it is not contrary to the requirements of the Fundamental Declarations that the three orders of sacred ministry shall be preserved by this Church.[119]

With the kinds of checks and balances proposed, even if the discussion was linked to questions of ministry, there is absolutely no threat to priesthood, or to episcopacy, or to Anglican Order at all.

And, if it is discussed in the proper context of the sacraments, then the threat is diminished even further. For a long time lay people have assisted the presbyters in their ministry by leading services and preaching, and the presbyter's role has remained intact. For a long time lay people have been enabled even to baptise in the case of necessity, but this is regarded as under the presbyter's delegation. The presbyter is appointed by the bishop to bring word and sacrament to the people. If the bishop delegates this ministry to the presbyter, then the ministry can be further delegated, and the presbyter's pastoral oversight is never diminished. And if a suitable lay person, duly authorised by the bishop, administers the Lord's Supper, as part of the means by which the needs of gospel ministry are met, then this, too, is no threat to the presbyter, but the lay person is always and only assisting the presbyter's ministry. After all, it is not the person who administers who renders the sacrament valid, it is the sacrament itself, a visible word that enshrines the promise of God. As the promise of God is received by faith, so the Spirit does the work of salvation in the believer.

ENDNOTES

1 See, for example, Carnley, *Reflections*, 158–159; Porter, *New Puritans*, 137–138; and the remarks of George Carey and Keith Rayner, reported in McGillion, *Chosen Ones*, 116, 168. Cf. Taylor, *Lay Presidency*, 7.

2 Taylor, *Lay Presidency*, 8.

3 Porter, *New Puritans*, 141, cf. 50: 'it is widely rumoured that it is informally happening in a number of Sydney parishes in any case'; Frame, *Anglicans in Australia*, 183: 'it was already being practiced unofficially in parts of the diocese. (The author remembers being at St Matthias' Church at Centennial Park when one such celebration was conducted in 1982)'.

4 Buchanan, 'Historical Perspectives', 13.

5 Freier, 'Kaparlgoo', 177. The clash occurred in November 1902.

6 Taylor, *Lay Presidency*, 9.

7 Carey, *Know the Truth*, 37.

8 General Synod, *Towards a Theology of Ordination*, 41.

9 Taylor, *Lay Presidency*, 7.

10 Stibbs, *Sacrament Sacrifice and Eucharist*; Beckwith, *Priesthood and Sacraments*, 30: 'If, therefore, the Church of England were now to make provision for laymen, when duly qualified and authorised, to exercise in appropriate circumstances not only the ministry of baptism or of the word but also of the Holy Communion, its action would not be alien to the historic Anglican formularies, but would on the contrary be a proper development of the principles which they embody'.

11 Synge, 'The Challenge of the Frontiers'.

12 Buchanan, 'Historical Perspectives', 16–17, 19.

13 Lloyd, *Lay Presidency at the Eucharist?*

14 Church of England in Australia, *Full Report (1971)*.

15 See House of Bishops, *Eucharistic Presidency*, 9; also Taylor, *Lay Presidency*, 8.

16 This development is reported by C. O. Buchanan in *News of Liturgy* 126 (1985), 3, but

Taylor, *Lay Presidency*, 8 n.13, comments that it 'appears otherwise to have passed unnoticed'.

17 Boff, 'Lay Co-ordinator'.

18 As reported by Colin Buchanan, 'Lay Administration Decision', noting that 'Lambeth 1998 went no further than Lambeth '88'.

19 Stott, *The Anglican Communion and Scripture*, 11.

20 Rosenthal & Currie, *Being Anglican [Report of 10th ACC]*, 2.5.

21 REFORM (Ireland), *Lay presidency at the Lord's Supper: opening a debate for the church* (1999), http://www.reform-ireland.org.uk/layceleb.htm.

22 Taylor, *Lay Presidency*, 8.

23 See the break-out box alongside Buchanan, 'Lay Administration Decision'.

24 'During the mediaeval period, the question of lay people celebrating Mass without a priest was raised, only to be dismissed, by the thirteenth century French Dominican scholar Guerric of St Quentin, as an exercise in scholastic casuistry', Taylor, *Lay Presidency*, 4. The recent debate began when the Dutch Dominicans circulated the booklet, 'Church and Ministry'. See 'Dutch Dominicans respond to priest shortage' 18 October 2007, http://www.liturgy.co.nz/worship/matters_files/dutchdominicans.html; and http://www.domlife.org/2007Stories/church_MinstryResponseDUTCH.html (24/8/2008).

25 The editors of the present volume are grateful to Nicholas Taylor for his generosity in supplying a pre-publication version, as well as for the gracious manner in which his book is written.

26 E.g. in 1999, Colin Buchanan spoke of an undoubted 'suspicion that Sydney is perversely opposed to anything which is elsewhere taken for granted without biblical basis. There is a kind of shrugging, "Oh, they would, wouldn't they?" response, which blunts the force of radical moves from Sydney. Sydney, on this view, is a school-girl who likes pulling her sister's hair just because it makes her cross. That is not my view, nor will it be easily recognisable in Sydney, but it is on the breeze'; 'Lay Administration Decision'. In 2004, Archbishop Jensen, felt the necessity to assure the clergy of Newcastle Diocese that Sydney were not proposing Lay Administration 'as a sort of payback' for other dioceses introducing the ordination of women; Jensen, 'Lay Administration (2004)', 1. In 2004, Carnley, *Reflections*, 164, after noting correctly that women could be involved in lay administration while headship of congregations is still reserved for men (Sydney's openly stated position), then says that 'some may find [this] more sinister'. In 2006, Porter, *New Puritans*, 138–139, declared: 'it is a hierarchical manoeuvre designed to achieve, once and for all, the Puritan objective of ridding the Church of ancient rituals and ceremonies'. Cf. Lloyd, *Lay Presidency?*, 5: 'none of us is discussing the anarchy of "lay presidency for anyone who wants it"'.

27 See the discussion of *The Ministration of Private Baptism of Children in Houses*, especially the third rubric, by Neil and Willoughby, *Tutorial Prayer Book*, 394–395, who conclude: 'the rubrics of 1549, 1552, and 1559 did not require Baptism to be administered by a clergyman, but in 1604 they were modified to exclude Lay Baptism'. The Sarum Manual even enjoined priests to give regular instruction to their people, in case they would be called upon to baptise. Not only has lay baptism 'been considered valid in the Church of England from the remotest times', but the English courts in the 1840s declared it valid, so much so that 'baptism rightly administered even by one in heresy and schism was valid'.

28 Taylor, *Lay Presidency*, 6.

29 Broughton, *A Charge* (1829), 15.

30 Broughton, *A Charge* (1829), 18.

31 Tertullian, *Exhortation to Chastity*, 7.30.

32 Taylor, *Lay Presidency*, 6–7.

33 For example, in 1997, the Scottish Episcopal Church produced a service entitled, *The Administration of Holy Communion from the Reserved Sacrament (when the Minister is a deacon or lay person*. Contrast Article XXVIII: The Sacrament of the Lord's Supper was not by Christ's ordinance reserved, carried about, lifted up, or worshipped; and cf. Article XXV.

34 See Allen, *Roland Allen*, 144–145, and Appendix 4.

35 http://www.lambethconference.org/resolutions/downloads/1930.pdf.

36 See, for example, the House of Bishops, *Eucharistic Presidency*, 61: 'In our own context, which is increasingly that of primary mission, the development of non-stipendiary priesthood in ministries of various kinds is proving to be a creative development'.

37 General Synod (ACA), *Towards a Theology of Ordination*, 41.

38 Cowper, *Barker*, 321, who comments that these men had officiated at several hundreds of services and this had greatly helped the work of the church.

39 Buchanan, 'Historical Perspectives', 13–14, speaks of the beginning of lay involvement in services in the parallel move in England, as lying behind the present issue. Readers were appointed in England from 1866; Taylor, *Lay Presidency*, 5.

40 Report on Lay Ministry and Licensing Thereto, Item 4(a), *Year Book 1977*, 317–318. Later the 'Local Lay Reader' emerged, who was not a member of the Association of Lay Readers. Under Archbishop Wright (1909), his role was clarified as being an assistant to the minister and the local lay reader had no permission to preach, a situation which technically prevailed through to the 1970s, even though it had become usual for local readers to preach.

41 Taylor, *Lay Presidency*, 7.

42 When speaking of structures that may be necessary 'to give clear guidance on what would and would not be a grave and lasting divisive course of action by a local church', Archbishop Williams stated: 'While at the moment the focus of this sort of question is sexual ethics, it could just as well be [amongst other things] about [...] lay presidency [...]'; *Second Presidential Address*. See also, Taylor, *Lay Presidency*, 261.

43 For example, McNeil, 'Body Image', 206, speaks of 'relationships between [Australian] dioceses strained almost to breaking point over issues such as the ordination of women, both as priests and bishops, the role of practising homosexuals within the life of the church and lay presidency of the eucharist'; Reid, 'Anglican Diversity', 249 (cf. 263) comments that, 'The Anglican Church of Australia is divided on at least three practical questions. There are different views with regard to the leadership of women in the church, to lay presidency at (or administration of) the eucharist, and to homosexuality'; Rayner, 'Historical and Global Contexts', 40, lists 'the ordination of women, homosexuality and proposals in Sydney for lay presidency at the eucharist' as the three notable new issues which threaten Australian Anglican unity; and Frame, 'Dynamics and Difficulties', 140, notes, 'Recent debates within the Anglican Church of Australia over expressions of human sexuality, ordination of women to the priesthood and the episcopate and lay presidency at the holy communion have strained the willingness of some Anglicans to be tolerant in matters, it is claimed, where compromise is impossible because the very character of Anglicanism is at stake'.

44 Porter, *New Puritans*, 137, cf. 137–148. Muriel Porter discusses the three issues together, she also adds that of divorce.

45 Porter, *New Puritans*, 137, cf. 137–148.

46 As noted by Carnley, *Reflections*, 156–157, 161–163; Hilliard, 'Pluralism', 140–141; and Taylor, *Lay Presidency*, 5–6, 258–259.

47 Frame, *Anglicans in Australia*, Ch. 7.

48 Frame, *Anglicans in Australia*, 201. According to Bishop Frame, Sydney's processes in the lay presidency show 'a capacity for generosity of spirit and a genuine regard for the divergent opinions of others within the Australian Church and the Anglican Communion', 182; 'the diocese has shown genuine regard for prevailing sentiment within the Anglican Communion by recognising and respecting the limits of diversity that the Communion would appear ready to tolerate. Such regard, however, has been noticeably absent in other parts of the Communion in relation to another controversial issue, a matter on which the Bible is far from silent', 188.

49 Such people would therefore fundamentally disagree with the statement that 'the ordination of women did not in any way alter the nature of the ministry and the liturgical life of the Church', Taylor, *Lay Presidency*, 262.

50 Carnley, *Reflections*, 158, speaks of a 'minor crisis of identity amongst those ordained to the ministerial priesthood', 'somehow there are fewer and fewer functions that fall exclusively and uniquely within the job description of a priest'.

51 Carnley, *Reflections*, 156–157, 161–163.

52 Addleshaw, 'The Law and Constitution', 74, comments that placing people on foreign soil under the Bishop of London was 'a policy which in practice was one of leaving them without any effective episcopal ministrations or government'. This situation prevailed until the first foreign bishopric was created, in Nova Scotia, at which time it became usual, from 1787 to 1867, for the Church of England to organise 'its members overseas in dioceses under Bishops appointed by Letters Patent from the Crown'.

53 In 1842, the dioceses of New Zealand and Tasmania were formed, followed by Adelaide, Newcastle and Melbourne in 1847. See http://www.anglican.org.nz/history.htm and Frame, 'the Anglican Church in Australia', http://www.anglican.org.au/index.cfm?SID=2&SSID=5&PID=6.

54 One such clergyman was probably Robert Allwood, who served at St James and whom Broughton named as one of his most supportive friends, and 'a pretty staunch Tractarian, but sound and cautious'. However, this led to only one point on which the two men 'had even an approach to difference of opinion', namely, 'as to the efficacy of ordinances administered by unqualified persons. Allwood seemed to hold their absolute invalidity, which I cannot bring myself to affirm: and he now appears more satisfied with the principle which is adopted by me in my Charge [i.e. of 1841]'; Broughton to Coleridge, 14th Feb 1842 (Moore College Library: Broughton Papers).

55 Broughton, *A Charge (1841)*.

56 Broughton, *A Charge (1841)*, 15–16.

57 Broughton, *A Charge (1841)*, 15–16.

58 Broughton, *A Charge (1841)*, 16–17.

59 Broughton, *A Charge (1841)*, 18.

60 Broughton, *A Charge (1841)*, 18.

61 Broughton, *A Charge (1841)*, 19.

62 Broughton, *A Charge (1841)*, 20.

63 Broughton, *A Charge (1841)*, 21.

64 Broughton, *A Charge (1841)*, 22.

65 This was the judgement made by the Arches Court, May 31, 1844, *Titchmarsh v Chapman*: 'baptism rightly administered even by one in heresy and schism was valid'.

66 Broughton, *Charge 1844*, 31.

67 Broughton, *Charge 1844*, 31–32.

68 Beckwith, *Priesthood and Sacraments*, 42, who cites William Whitaker as 'the only representative divine of the period who takes the opposite view'.

69 Beckwith, *Priesthood and Sacraments*, 42–43.

70 Beckwith, *Priesthood and Sacraments*, 43.

71 Beckwith, *Priesthood and Sacraments*, 43–44; 'The decisions of the courts turned mainly upon the alterations to the Prayer Book service of private baptisms, which were made in 1604 and mostly confirmed in 1662: were these alterations intended to prohibit laymen from officiating at the service, or merely to express a clear preference for a clergyman, as being the norm […] King James I, who was mainly responsible for the changes, stated that baptism by laymen or by women was not prohibited, any more than it was authorised, by the 1604 service, and the courts, no doubt rightly, judged this to be the true interpretation' (p.44).

72 Beckwith, *Priesthood and Sacraments*, 44.

73 The fact that the Puritan party rejected lay baptism and lay administration, introduces an irony in the contemporary debate, at the expence of Muriel Porter, *The New Puritans*, 50, 137–148, who has identified the press towards lay administration as a sign of Sydney's supposed 'Puritanism'!

74 Beckwith, *Priesthood and Sacraments*, 45.

75 Beckwith, *Priesthood and Sacraments*, 45.

76 A Charter was granted to the East India Company in 1600, and it founded a trading post at Surat in 1614, and gradually grew in power and influence. Despite early hostility from the Dutch, the English had full control of Madras by 1640, Bombay by 1662, and Calcutta in 1690. Higgins, *One Faith and Fellowship*, 130–132. For the history of the early missions in India, see Allen & McClure, *Two Hundred Years [SPCK]*, Ch. 8.

77 Higgins, *One Faith and Fellowship*, 132.

78 Allen & McClure, *Two Hundred Years [SPCK]*, 258. The first two were Bartholemew Ziegenbalg and Henry Plutschau, who set out for India on 29 November 1705, and arrived at Tranquebar 19 July 1706. SPCK was invited to assist the mission in about 1709, and its members did so very warmly; pp.259–60.

79 Allen & McClure, *Two Hundred Years [SPCK]*, 263.

80 Allen & McClure, *Two Hundred Years [SPCK]*, 261.

81 Allen & McClure, *Two Hundred Years [SPCK]*, 262.

82 Allen & McClure, *Two Hundred Years [SPCK]*, 265.

83 Allen & McClure, *Two Hundred Years [SPCK]*, 266.

84 Allen & McClure, *Two Hundred Years [SPCK]*, 275–276.

85 Higgins, *One Faith and Fellowship*, 132.

86 Allen & McClure, *Two Hundred Years [SPCK]*, 280.

87 Allen & McClure, *Two Hundred Years [SPCK]*, 284–285.

88 We read in the minutes for December 4, 1744, "Recommended to ye Missionaries to continue ye use of ye Ch. Of Eng. Catechism, and to Baptize in ye form of Com. Prayer.'", Allen & McClure, *Two Hundred Years [SPCK]*, 266, n. *.

89 Allen & McClure, *Two Hundred Years [SPCK]*, 265. Aaron was ordained in 1733, Diogo in 1741, and 'both of these natives gained many converts', then in 1790, Sattianaden was ordained with the sanction of the Society, who then published the sermon he preached on the occasion, to aid the publicity of the mission. Missionary Schwartz ordained his foster-son, John Caspar Kohlhoff in 1787. See also Lowther-Clark, *The History of the S.P.C.K.*, 64, who gives the year as 1784, which was when permission was requested of the Society.

90 Lowther-Clark, *The History of the S.P.C.K.*

91 Lowther-Clark, *The History of the S.P.C.K.*, 64.

92 Neill, *Anglicanism*, 213–214.

93 Neill, *Anglicanism*, 214.

94 Neill, *Anglicanism*, 215–216.

95 Cnattingius, *Bishops and Societies*, Chs. 3 & 5.

96 Neill, *Anglicanism*, 214.

97 See, for example, Peck, *Anglicanism and Episcopacy*, 40. For further comments on the Indian situation, see pp.45–51.

98 Heber died untimely in 1826, and was followed by Bishops James and Turner, after whom 'the great Daniel Wilson' arrived to the See of Calcutta in 1832; Higgins, *One Faith and Fellowship*, 134.

99 Sykes, *Old Priest*, 164.

100 Sykes, *Old Priest*, 166; Lowther-Clark, *The History of the S.P.C.K.*, 64.

101 Sykes, *Old Priest*, 167, citing Heber, *Narrative*, 3.411.

102 Addleshaw, 'Law and Constitution', 82. No Bishop of Calcutta ever visited this furthest part of his Diocese, even though some, such as Daniel Wilson, sought to take their responsibilities seriously, through correspondence and through having his charge read in Sydney; cf. Micklem, *Australia's First Bishop*, 15.

103 Broughton to Coleridge, 19 Oct 1837 (Moore College: Broughton Papers); also reproduced in Bailey, *Twenty-Five Years*, 13.

104 Micklem, *Australia's First Bishop*, 14.

105 Cited by Broughton in the Appendix B, *Charge (1841)*, 37–38.

106 Taylor, *Lay Presidency*, 7.

107 Synge, 'Challenge', 157.

108 Broughton, *A Charge (1841)*, 16–17.

109 Synge, 'Challenge', 159.

110 Synge, 'Challenge', 160.

111 Synge, 'Challenge', 161.

112 Synge, 'Challenge', 161.

113 Synge, 'Challenge', 162.

114 For one examination of Sydney Diocese, see Judd & Cable, *Sydney Anglicans*.

115 Carnley, *Reflections*, 167–176. This two-view schema can be criticised for not giving sufficient weight to the presbyter as the teacher of God's word to whom congregational oversight has been committed.

116 Robinson, 'Presidency and Assistance', 400.

117 Cf. Taylor, *Lay Presidency*, 9.

118 See Carnley, *Reflections*, 164.

119 Bishop of Bathurst, Reasons, *Appellate Tribunal Opinion. Reference Concerning Lay and Diaconal Presidency (7 March 1996)*, 87; Cf. Justice Handley's similar reasoning, p.22.

6

Some concluding thoughts

ROBERT TONG

The question

The chapters in this book have sought to answer the question: Is a presbyter essential for the due administration of the Lord's Supper? For evangelicals the prior question is 'what does the Bible say?' Next, as the activity takes place within a congregation, we must ask 'is it edifying?' Lastly, because this is an issue in an Anglican context, we ask 'is it true to Anglican principles?'

As long ago as the 14th century, a Lollard put the question like this, 'No priest has power to make Christ's body in the form of bread in the sacrament of the altar'.[1]

In more recent times, a Vice-Principal of Oak Hill Theological College commented:

> There are other matters of great practical importance concerning the administration of this sacrament, in which there are room and urgent need for a fuller obedience to the teaching and the principles of God's written Word. Let us indicate some of them.
>
> First, since some one person present in any congregation must take the lead in administering the Lord's Supper, the question still

needs to be faced—by whom may the Holy Communion be administered? The proper Christian answer is surely, in principle, by any member whom the body of believers may entrust with this ministry. There is no doctrinal necessity with Holy Communion, any more than there is with baptism, that one class of special ministers alone may administer it. Also, while it is, on the one hand, important that, as a corporate activity of the local church, its administration should be carefully ordered and entrusted only to responsible elders, yet there is, on the other hand, great practical need for an increase in the number of those who are thus allowed to do it. Why, for the lack of a bishop or presbyter, should congregations be deprived of the Lord's Supper, when they have in their midst godly members, who could, if given the opportunity, worthily fulfil the necessary ministry? Why should such Christians be allowed as lay readers to lead public worship and to preach the Word in the congregation but not to administer the Lord's Supper? Would it not increase in any congregation the awareness of equality and brotherhood and common unworthiness if different senior members, duly authorised or ordained as elders, administered the sacrament in turn? Also, it is time that, by practice as well as by words, we found ways to confess our conviction that there is in the New Testament no indication that proper administration can be performed only by someone who has been admitted to a special sacerdotal order of ministry.[2]

Over the last few years I have had more than a score of conversations with Anglicans of 'all sorts and conditions' from various parts of the world about the question at issue.[3] In every case, after time was spent in vigorous conversation, there was agreement that the fundamental proposition was not contrary to Scripture. Opposition was always couched in terms of Anglo-Catholic ecclesiology and theology.[4]

So it was no surprise to find a quite recent (2005) English publication reporting that it was 'universally accepted that there is no explicit New Testament teaching about who should preside at the Eucharist'.[5] And citing in support the English House of Bishops' *Eucharistic Presidency* report:[6]

as far as eucharistic presidency is concerned, there is no indication anywhere in the New Testament of an explicit link between the Church's office and presiding at the Eucharist. There is certainly no attempt to link theologically the discernment of charismatic gifts and the developing notions of office with particular powers, functions or responsibilities with respect to the Eucharist. There is no suggestion that anyone was ordained or appointed to an office which consisted primarily of saying the blessing over the bread and wine.

Unfortunately, and in line with the experience of my own conversations, the report goes on to defend at length, and as the traditional position in the Church of England, arguments anchored in the Anglo-Catholic tradition.

Authorised services

As a bulwark against heresy and to maintain church order the English Parliament rigidly regulated the liturgy permitted for use in the Church of England.[7] A concession from liturgical uniformity was granted by Edward Vl to the so called 'Stranger Churches' of Protestant refugees fleeing persecution on the Continent.[8] This concession was renewed by Elizabeth l. As a consequence of the 1662 *Act of Uniformity,* Dissent became a permanent feature of the mainstream ecclesiastical landscape and national liturgical uniformity was lost, never to be recovered.

At this point it is worth summarising the canonical foundations for the various forms of service authorised for use in the Diocese of Sydney. In Australia for most of the first two hundred years Anglicans were liturgically constrained, at least as a matter of law, by the principles of the *Act of Uniformity.* The *Red Book Case*[9] underscored the reality of this liturgical straight jacket. During the 1950s, members of the twenty five diocesan synods and the General Synod voted on the constitutional place of *The Book of Common Prayer* in the life of the proposed new independent Australian church.[10]

After a gestation of nearly fifty years the Australian Church had a constitution which enshrined *The Book of Common Prayer* together with the *Thirty-nine Articles*:

> as the authorised standard of worship and doctrine in this church
> and no alteration in, or permitted variations from the services or
> articles therein contained shall contravene any principal of
> doctrine or worship laid down in such standard.[11]

Section 4 of the Constitution goes on to allow a bishop of a diocese
to permit deviations from the existing orders of service 'which do not
contravene any principal of doctrine or worship'. Any variations must
be submitted to the bishop by the incumbent and churchwardens of
a parish, after the majority of parishioners have voted at a meeting of
parishioners. It was the *Red Book Case* which shaped these variation
provisions.

One driving force in the adoption of a constitution was the
growing demand for Prayer Book revision. After much careful work,
in which Bishop Donald Robinson played a major part, the 1978
General Synod authorised for use *An Australian Prayer Book*. It was
quickly taken up by every diocese, *for use together with the Book of
Common Prayer 1662*. When in 1995, after an acrimonious debate, the
General Synod authorised for use, *A Prayer Book for Australia*, the
Sydney Synod declined to adopt it and therefore none of the services
contained in that book are generally available for use in that diocese.
When some parishes have applied for specific approval for specific
services, approval has been granted by the Archbishop pursuant to
section 4 of the Constitution.

Section 4 has also been used to sanction various experimental
services published by the diocesan liturgical committee.

The prospect of creating new services and the ease of variations to
old, became possible in 1998 when Sydney synod adopted the General
Synod *Canon Concerning Services 1992*.[12] Thereafter a minister was
authorised to make variations to authorised services, which were not of
substantial importance. Clause 5 contained a time bomb identified by
Canon Bruce Ballantine-Jones.[13] A minister can now construct suitable

forms of service for occasions where no provision has been made in the authorised liturgical texts. Any new service is required to be reverent and edifying and not contrary to the doctrine of the Anglican Church of Australia. A parishioners' meeting and the agreement of the bishop, as provided by section 4 of the Constitution, is no longer necessary. Family, youth or outreach services could be an *occasion for which no provision* is made in the existing library of authorised services. The spectre of the *Red Book Case* as far as conformity to the text of *The Book of Common Prayer* is put to rest. Within the doctrinal boundaries of the Constitution and the requirement for edification, there are enormous possibilities for engaging the people of God when they meet in public assembly.

The road ahead

Implementing the affirmation that the Lord's Supper in the Diocese of Sydney may be administered by persons other than presbyters will bring about no immediate visible change. Where robed clergy lead the public services of a parish there is no visible distinction in the clerical dress of deacons or presbyters.[14] Where the service leaders are in common attire then there is no visible difference between a lay leader, deacon or presbyter. As to formal title, both deacon and presbyter are 'Reverend'.

At another level within parish life, synodical "permission" is given for pastoral visitors to the sick and aged, home groups, fellowship groups, scripture teaching in schools groups, weekends away and the like to share the Lord's Supper in appropriate circumstances without the need for a presbyter. In fact there is a distinct practical advantage to this initiative as the extent of ministry in a parish is usually beyond the reach of one incumbent. It is unrealistic to expect the incumbent to be fully involved in every aspect of parish life. Where mission or outreach is on the front foot in a parish, there will be new house groups, church plants and other meetings held outside church buildings and off parish property. Lay leadership will be heavily involved in all aspects of a busy mission minded parish. Additionally, Anglican Christians meet for ministry and fellowship in many places outside the parish structure: at work, at play, in schools, in hospitals, in gaols and many other places where two or three are gathered.

Where the Lord's Supper is appropriate,[15] the Anglo-catholic response is extended communion, which others feel is still subject to the same objections as reservation of the sacrament. In an evangelical theological setting, a different answer is required.

The question again or is it Anglican?

The rich diversity of Anglicanism has already proved able to tolerate lay administration in the past, in situations of missionary expansion and other necessity. Two examples will suffice. During the eighteenth and early nineteenth centuries, all the 28 missionaries serving under SPCK in India were in Lutheran Orders. They 'baptised children and celebrated the Holy Communion according to the Anglican rite'.[16] Secondly, when Archbishop George Carey was serving his national service with the RAF in Iraq, he and several friends held church services and 'I celebrated Holy Communion—quite illegally of course. I don't suppose that the Almighty was bothered that in the absence of a Priest, that a group of young men took it in turns to use the words of the 1662 Prayer Book and to celebrate Communion'.[17]

In a review of an Anglican-Methodist church union report, Roger Beckwith[18] considered why the English Reformers retained the custom that only bishops and presbyters should administer the Holy Communion. He concluded:

> that it is theologically unexceptionable, at any rate in cases of need, for laymen to preach the word, to baptise, or to administer the Holy Communion, provided they are duly authorised and so are acting in an auxiliary capacity, not usurping the office of the clergymen. The fact that they made no provision for exceptions, save the customary provision for the case of emergency baptism, only means that when

the Prayer Book was drawn up there was a great deal of ignorance and illiteracy among the laity and no shortage of clergy whereas today there is a shortage, not only among the Methodists and in many overseas Anglican dioceses but also in the Church of England. If therefore, the Church of England were now to make provision for laymen, when duly qualified and authorised, to exercise in appropriate circumstances not only the ministry of baptism or of the word but also of the Holy Communion, its action would not be alien to the historic Anglican formularies but would, on the contrary, be a proper development of the principles which they embody.[19]

The issue of lay and diaconal administration is an issue the Diocese of Sydney has been wrestling with for more than thirty years. We consider it to be a development which is true to Anglican principles, as outlined by the 2008 Jerusalem Declaration.

We, together with many other faithful Anglicans throughout the world, believe the doctrinal foundation of Anglicanism, which defines our core identity as Anglicans, is expressed in these words: The doctrine of the Church is grounded in the Holy Scriptures and in such teachings of the ancient Fathers and Councils of the Church as are agreeable to the said Scriptures. In particular, such doctrine is to be found in the Thirty-nine Articles of Religion, the Book of Common Prayer and the Ordinal.[20]

If the practice were a matter of doctrine, then the teaching of the Bible alone would be determinative. However the Bible is silent on the issue. If the practice were a matter of order, then it would need to be consistent with the teaching of the Bible, the doctrine of the Thirty-nine Articles and the principles of the Book of Common Prayer. With respect to the latter, the Appellate Tribunal[21] has expressed the opinion that the practice of lay and diaconal administration is consistent with the teaching of the Bible, the doctrine of the Thirty-nine Articles and the principles of The Book of Common Prayer.[22]

While other Anglicans may not agree with our views on this issue, we believe that, although a secondary matter, lay and diaconal administration could certainly take its place amongst the rich diversity of practice within Anglicanism. As the Jerusalem Declaration expresses it:

> We celebrate the God-given diversity among us which enriches our global fellowship, and we acknowledge freedom in secondary matters. We pledge to work together to seek the mind of Christ on issues that divide us.[23]

It is our hope that those who disagree with our views will in a spirit of generosity and freedom accept such differences in secondary matters within the Anglican Communion, as together we continue to seek the mind of Christ.

ENDNOTES

1   Cross, *Church and People*, 2.

2   Stibbs, *Sacrament, Sacrifice and Eucharist*, 85.

3   These opportunities have arisen at a number of Anglican Consultative Council meetings, Lambeth 1998, and the Archbishop of Canterbury's Panel of Reference.

4   Ecumenical conversations between Anglicans and other Protestants usually disclose Anglican insistence on the Historic Episcopate and the administration of the Lord's Supper only by episcopally ordained presbyters. These two issues were evident in Church of England-Methodist conversations in the 1950s and surface again in the report cited in the next footnote. Roger Beckwith provides a critical and penetrating evangelical analysis of these issues in *Priesthood and Sacraments*.

5   Joint Implementation Commission, *In The Spirit of The Covenant* para 6.4.38.

6   House of Bishops, *Eucharistic Presidency* para 4.20.

7   See the several *Acts of Uniformity* passed in 1549, 1552, 1559 and 1662 enforcing *The Book of Common Prayer* as the only authorised liturgy in the Church of England.

8   Pettegree, *Foreign Protestant Communities*.

9   *Wylde v Attorney General (NSW)* (1948) 78 CLR 224 decided that where a service of Holy Communion was not conducted in strict conformity to the service printed in *The Book of Common Prayer* then it was a breach of the trusts on which the church land was held, and injunctions were granted to restrain the illegal use.

10   From the time of English settlement in 1788 until 1961, Anglicans in Australia were, in law, part of the Church of England. *The Church of England in Australia* (from 1976 known as the *Anglican Church of Australia*) came into independent existence on 1 January 1962. See Davis, *Australian Anglicans and their Constitution*.

11   Section 4 of the *Constitution of the Anglican Church of Australia*, which is set out as a Schedule to the *Anglican Church of Australia Constitution Act 1961*(NSW). The other States of

Australia have similar but not identical covering Acts which annex the Constitution as a schedule. For full text of section 4 see page 43 in present text.

12 For ease of reference sections 4 & 5 are set out

4. (1) The following forms of service are authorised:–
   (a) The forms of service contained in the Book of Common Prayer.
   (b) Such forms as may have been authorised, as regards a parish, pursuant to the Constitution or a canon of the General Synod in force in the diocese of which that parish is part.

   (2) Every minister must use only the authorised forms of service except so far as the minister may exercise the discretion allowed by section 5.

5. (1) The minister may make and use variations which are not of substantial importance in any form of service authorised by section 4 according to particular circumstances.

   (2) Subject to any regulation made from time to time by the Synod of a diocese, a minister of that diocese may, on occasions for which no provision is made, use forms of service considered suitable by the minister for those occasions.

   (3) All variations in forms of service and all forms of service used must be reverent and edifying and must not be contrary to or a departure from the doctrine of this Church.

   (4) A question concerning the observance of the provisions of sub-section 5(3) may be determined by the bishop of the diocese.

13 Ballantine-Jones, 'A Quiet Revolution'; See also *Southern Cross* July, August and September 1999 where Bishop Donald Robinson challenges the claimed width of the new provision and Neil Cameron, a former member of the General Synod Canon Law Commission, rebuts it.

14 *The Book of Common Prayer and the Canons* of 1604 only require deacons and presbyters to wear a surplice and hood 'as are agreeable to their degrees'.

15 We have not in this book addressed the matter of frequency of administration. The parish communion movement and the Oxford movement have increased the demand but this was not always the case. See for example, Hunt, 'The Lord's Supper in Early Modern England'.

16 Neill, *Anglicanism*, 213. Before the creation of the Diocese of Australia (in 1836, under Bishop Broughton), the Sydney colonial outpost was part of the vast Diocese of Calcutta. Does this mean that administration of the Lord's Supper by persons not episcopally ordained was already happening in the diocese?

17 Carey, *Know the Truth*, 37.

18 At the time of writing the book cited in the next footnote, Beckwith held the office of Librarian at Latimer House Oxford. J I Packer was the Warden and John Stott the Chairman of Council. Beckwith was awarded a DD by Archbishop George Carey and was a participant at GAFCON 2008.

19 Beckwith, *Priesthood and Sacraments*, 29.

20 http://www.gafcon.org/index.php?option=com_content&task=view&id=79&Itemid=31.

21 The Appellate Tribunal is established by the Anglican Church of Australia constitution as the final internal appeal tribunal for matters of clergy discipline and issues of faith ritual and ceremonial. Additionally, it has an advisory opinion function for questions arising under the constitution.

22 Reference Concerning Diaconal and Lay Presidency (7 March 1996).

23 Paragraph 12 of the *Jerusalem Declaration*.

Bibliography

1. Sydney Diocese Publications

a. Year Books

Each issue of the *Year Book of the Diocese of Sydney* is cited by the year of publication, but each contains the reports of the Synod for the year prior to publication.

Details of synods from 1993 to 2007 can be accessed through http://www.sds.asn.au/Site/100818.asp?ph=sy.

Reports can be found at http://www.sds.asn.au/site/102954.asp?ph=sy.

b. Reports

1977 • Synod Committee, *Re The Meaning, Value and Theology of Ordination* (1977), *Year Book 1978*, 348–349. Also printed in *Southern Cross* (February, 1979), 15.

1978 • Synod Committee, *Re The Meaning, Value and Theology of Ordination* (1978). Printed in *Southern Cross* (February, 1979), 16, 21–24.

1983 • Diocesan Doctrine Commission (1983), *Re 11/81 "Towards a Theology of Ordination" Year Book of 1984*, 366–374.

1984 • Diocesan Doctrine Commission (1984), *Re Synod Resolution 37/83 "Towards a Theology of Ordination", Year Book 1985*, 452–459.

1985 • Synod Committee, *Re 37/83 "Towards a Theology of Ordination": Lay Presidency at the Holy Communion Year Book 1986*, 314–316.

1986 • Standing Committee, Re *18/85 Lay Presidency at Holy Communion, Year Book 1987*, 258–259.

1986 • Synod Committee, Re *Lay Presidency at the Holy Communion, Year Book 1988*, 327–330.

1987 • Standing Committee Legal Committee, *Re Lay Presidency at the Holy Communion, Year Book 1988*, 330–334.

1993 • Diocesan Doctrine Commission (1993): *Lay Presidency at the Lord's Supper, Year Book 1994*, 459–469.

1993 • Diocesan Doctrine Commission (1993): *Diaconal Presidency at the Lord's Supper*, *Year Book 1994*, 409–422.

1994 • Standing Committee Sub-Committee, *Re 16/94 Lay and Diaconal Administration of the Lord's Supper, Year Book 1995*, 427–444.

1995 • Diocesan Doctrine Commission (1995): *Lay and Diaconal Administration of the Lord's Supper, Year Book 1996*, 422–430.

1998 • Diocesan Doctrine Commission (1998): *Lay and Diaconal Administration of the Lord's Supper, Year Book 1999*, 449–459.

1999 • '34/98: Lay and Diaconal Administration of the Holy Communion', report for Standing Committee, *Year Book 2000*, 490–492.

1999 • 'The Archbishop's Statement', *Southern Cross* (December, 1999), 4.

2003 • '25/01: Lay and Diaconal Administration of the Lord's Supper', Report to Standing Committee, *Year Book 2004*, 392–401.

2007 • Standing Committee, *Re 26/03 Lay and Diaconal Administration of Holy Communion? Legal Impediments.* http://www.sds.asn.au/Site/103716.asp?ph=sy.

2. General Synod and Other Anglican Reports

1559 • *'Elizabeth's Act of Uniformity* (1559), *1Elizabeth*, Cap. 2', H. Gee & W.J. Hardy (eds.), Documents Illustrative of English Church History (New York: Macmillan, 1896), 458–67. http://history.hanover.edu/texts/engref/er80.html.

1603 • *Constitutions and Canons Ecclesiastical: (made in the year 1603 and amended in the years 1865, 1887, 1936, 1946, and 1948)* (London: SPCK, 1961).

1930 • Lambeth Conference 1930, http://www.lambethconference.org/resolutions/downloads/1930.pdf.

1963 • *1963 Anglican Congress. Report of Proceedings. August 13–23 Toronto, Canada* (E.R. Fairweather, ed.; Toronto: Editorial Committee, 1963).

1971 • Church of England in Australia, *Full report of the Conference on Mission and Ministry: including a selection of the introductory papers and addresses* (Canberra, A.C.T: Lowes, for the Conference, 1971).

1977 • General Synod (ACA), *General Synod 1977: Reports* (Sydney: General Synod, 1977). *Proceedings of the Fifth General Synod, 1977* (Sydney: General Synod, 1978).

1981 • General Synod Commission on Doctrine, *Towards a Theology of Ordination* (Sydney: Standing Committee of General Synod, 1981).

1983 • Report of the Advisory Council for the Church's Ministry, to General Synod (C of E) November 1983. J. Tiller, *A Strategy for the Church's Ministry* (Westminster: CIO, for the ACCM, 1983).

1989 • *Reports to General Synod (8th)* (Sydney: General Synod, 1989), Vol. 1.

1992 • *Reports to General Synod (9th)* (Sydney: General Synod, 1992),Vol. 1.

1995 • *Lay Presidency at the Eucharist: A Theological Consultation* (Sydney: Standing Committee of General Synod, 1995).

1995 • Melbourne Commission on Lay Presidency, *Presidency at the Eucharist.*

1995 • *Tenth General Synod 1995.* Vol. 1: *Reports* (Sydney: General Synod, 1995).

1996 • I. Head (ed.), *Who May Celebrate? Boundaries of Anglican Order* (Sydney: General Synod Standing Committee, 1996).

1997 • Scottish Episcopal Church, *The Administration of Holy Communion from the Reserved Sacrament (when the Minister is a deacon or lay person* (Edinburgh: General Synod of Scottish Episcopal Church, 1997).

1997 • House of Bishops (Church of England), *Eucharistic Presidency. A Theological Statement by the House of Bishops of the General Synod* (London: Church House, 1997).

1997 • J. Rosenthal & N. Currie (eds.), *Being Anglican in the Third Millennium. Panama 1996. The Official Report of the 10th Meeting of the Anglican Consultative Council* (Harrisburg: Morehouse, 1997).

1998 • *The Eleventh General Synod 1998.* Book 4: *Reports* (Sydney: General Synod, 1998).

1998 • Anglican Church of Australia, *Appellate Tribunal Opinion. Reference Concerning Lay and Diaconal Presidency (7 March 1996)* (Sydney: General Synod, 1998).

1999 • REFORM (Ireland), *Lay presidency at the Lord's Supper : opening a debate for the church* (1999). http://www.reform-ireland.org.uk/layceleb.htm.

2001 • House of Bishops (Church of England), *For Such a Time as This: A Renewed Diaconate in the Church of England: a report to the General Synod of the Church of England of a working party of the House of Bishops* (London: Church House, 2001).

2006 • Archbishop of Canterbury's Pastoral Letter, March 2006. See http://www.lambeth conference.org/lc2008/news/news.cfm?mode=entry&entry=0EF2A684-EE2D-9FA2-F5CAA03F0133AE3E

2007 • *Anglican Church of Australia General Synod, Appellate Tribunal Opinion. Reference concerning Women Bishops (22 April, 2005)* (Sydney: General Synod, 2007). See http://www.anglican.org.au/docs/ATWomenBishop270907.pdf.

2008 • Archbishop Rowan Williams, *Presidential Address to the Lambeth Conference 2008 (20th July)*, http://www.archbishopofcanterbury.org/media/pdf/n/0/Lambeth_20 opening_20address.pdf.

2007 • 'Dutch Dominicans respond to priest shortage' 18 October 2007, http://www.liturgy.co.nz/worship/matters_files/dutchdominicans.html; and http://www.domlife.org/2007Stories/church_MinstryResponseDUTCH.html (24/8/2008).

2008 • Archbishop Rowan Williams, *Second Presidential Address to the Lambeth Conference 2008 (29th July)*, http://www.lambethconference.org/daily/news.cfm/2008/7/29/ ACNS4487.

2008 • GAFCON, Jerusalem Statement. http://www.gafcon.org/index.php?option=com_ content&task=view&id=79&Itemid=31.

3. Other Works Referred To

a. Archival Material

Moore College: Broughton Papers:
> Broughton to E. Coleridge, 19 Oct 1837.
>> This letter is also reproduced in Bailey, *Twenty-Five Years*, 11–17.
> Broughton to E. Coleridge, 14 Feb 1842.

St Andrew's house
> Provincial Synod Papers
>> Report of the Lay-Presidency Group, to Standing Committee, Nov. 1990

b. Other Works

Adam, P. • 'A theological case for Lay Presidency' (Unpublished discussion paper for General Synod Commission on Doctrine, 1990).

Addleshaw, G.W.O. • 'The Law and Constitution of the Church Overseas', in E.R. Morgan & R. Lloyd (eds.), *The Mission of the Anglican Communion* (London: SPCK & SPG, 1948), 74–98.

Allen, H.J.B. • *Roland Allen. Pioneer, Priest, and Prophet* (Cincinatti & Grand Rapids: Forward Movement & Eerdmans, 1995).

Allen, R. • *The Case for Voluntary Clergy* (London: Eyre & Spottiswoode, 1930).

Allen, W.O.B. & E. McClure, • *Two Hundred Years: The History of The Society for Promoting Christian Knowledge, 1698–1898* (London: SPCK, 1898).

Australian Church Record, • 'Lay Administration Bill Founders on Standing Orders', *Australian Church Record* 1878 (1 Feb 1999), 9.

Bailey, H. • *Twenty-Five Years at St. Augustine's College: a letter to late students* ([Canterbury?]: printed for the Warden of St. Augustine's, by S. Hyde, 1873).

Ballantine-Jones, B. • 'A Quiet Revolution', *Anglican Church League News* (June 1999). Ballantine-Jones replied to responses to this article in *Southern Cross* (September, 1999), 19.

Beckwith, R.T. • *Priesthood and Sacraments. A Study in the Anglican-Methodist Report* (Latimer Monographs 1; Appleford: Marcham Manor, 1964).

Boff, L. • 'The Lay Co-ordinator and the Celebration of the Lord's Supper', Ecclesiogenesis. The Base Communities Reinvent the Church (R.R. Barr, transl.; London: Collins, 1986), Ch. 6.

Broughton, W. G. • *A Charge, Delivered to the Clergy of the Archdeaconry of New South Wales, at the Primary Visitation, holden at Sydney, in the Church of St James, on Thursday, the 3d of December, 1829* (Sydney: R. Mansfield for executors of R. Howe, 1830). Now bound with *Broughton's Sermons &c.* (Moore College Library).

Broughton, W. G. • *A Charge, delivered to the Clergy of New South Wales, at the Visitation held in the Church of St James, Sydney, on Wednesday, October the 6th, 1841, by William Grant Broughton, D.D., Bishop of Australia* (Sydney: James Tegg, 1841).

Broughton, W. G. • *A Charge, to the Clergy of the Diocese of Australia, by William Grant, Lord Bishop of Australia, delivered at the Triennial Visitation in May, 1844* (Sydney: Kemp & Fairfax, 1844).

Buchanan, C. • 'Some Anglican Historical Perspectives', in Lloyd, Lay Presidency?, 11–19.

Buchanan, C. • 'Lay Administration Decision—An English View', *Southern Cross* (December 1999), 7.

Cameron, N. • 'Passion Burns for Church's Quiet Revolution', *Southern Cross* (September, 1999), 18–19.

Carey, G. • *Know the Truth* (London: Harper Collins, 2003).

Carnley, P. • 'A Response to "Lay Presidency at the Lord's Supper", A Report of the Diocesan Doctrine Commission of the Anglican Diocese of Sydney', (Unpublished discussion paper presented to the Sydney Diocesan Doctrine Commission 1994).

Chapman, J. C. • 'Lay Presidency at the Holy Communion', in *Agenda for a Biblical Church: 2. Debates and Issues from the National Evangelical Anglican Conference* (Sydney: AIO, 1981), 104–5.

Cnattingius, H. • *Bishops and Societies. A Study of Anglican Colonial and Missionary Expansion 1698–1850* (London: SPCK, 1952).

Cowper, W.M. • *The Episcopate of the Right Reverend Frederic Barker D.D., Bishop of Sydney and Metropolitan of Australia: A Memoir* (London: Hatchards, 1888).

Cranmer, Thomas • *A Defence of the True and Catholick Doctrine of the Sacrament*, Book V, Chapter XI: *The difference between the priest and the layman* (Lewes, E. Sussex: Focus Christian Ministries Trust, 1987).

Cross, C. • *Church and People, England 1450-1660* (Oxford: Blackwell, ^{2}1999).

Davis, J • *Australian Anglicans and their Constitution* (Canberra: Acorn, 1993).

Frame, T. • 'The Dynamics and Difficulties of Debate in Australian Anglicanism', in T. Frame & G. Treloar (eds.), *Agendas for Australian Anglicanism. Essays in honour of Bruce Kaye* (Adelaide: ATF, 2006), 139–169.

Frame, T. • *Anglicans in Australia* (Sydney: University of NSW, 2007).

Frame, T. • 'The Anglican Church in Australia', http://www.anglican.org.au/index.cfm?SID =2&SSID=5&PID=6

Freier, P. • 'Kaparlgoo: A Pattern for Anglican Arnhem Land "Industrial Missions"', in P. Carroll & S. Etherington (eds.), One Land, One Saviour (Sydney: CMS, 2008), 160–181.

Head, I. (ed.) • 'Introduction', *Who May Celebrate? Boundaries of Anglican Order* (Sydney: Standing Committee of General Synod, 1996), 1–3.

Heber, R. • *Narrative of a Journey through the Upper Provinces from Calcutta to Bombay, 1824–1825, (with notes upon Ceylon), an account of a journey to Madras and the southern provinces, 1826, and letters written in India* (London: J. Murray, 1828).

Higgins, J.S. • *One Faith and Fellowship: The Missionary Story of the Anglican Communion* (London: Seabury, 1958).

Hilliard, D. • 'Pluralism and New Alignments in Society and Church', in B.L. Kaye (ed.), *Anglicanism in Australia. A History* (Melbourne: Melbourne University Press, 2002), 124–148.

Hooker, R. • *Lawes of Ecclesiasticall Politie* (London: Dent, repr. 1907).

Hunt, A. • 'The Lord's Supper in Early Modern England', *Past and Present* 161 (November, 1998), 39–83.

Jensen, P.F. • 'Lay Administration of the Holy Communion', Unpublished Address to the Clergy Conference, Anglican Diocese of Newcastle, 19 February 2004.

Joint Implementation Commission, • *In The Spirit of The Covenant. Interim Report of the Joint Implementation Commission under the Covenant between The Methodist Church of Great Britain and the Church of England* (Peterborough: Methodist Publishing, 2005). See also http://www.anglican-methodist.org.uk.

Joint Implementation Commission, • *Living God's Covenant – Second Interim Report (2007) of the Joint Implementation Commission (JIC) under the Covenant between the Methodist Church of Great Britain and the Church of England.* www.sheffield.anglican.org/documents/s%20 Covenant-2nd%20Interim%20Report.doc (24/8/2008).

Judd, S. & K.J. Cable, • *Sydney Anglicans. A History of the Diocese* (Sydney: AIO, 1987).

Kaye, B.L. (ed.) • *'Wonderful and Confessedly Strange'. Australian Essays in Anglican Ecclesiology* (Adelaide: Australian Theological Forum, 2006).

Lightfoot, J. B. • *St Paul's Epistle to the Philippians* (London: Macmillan, 1903).

Lloyd, T. (ed.) • *Lay Presidency at the Eucharist?* (Grove Liturgical Studies 9; Bramcote: Grove, 1977).

Lowther-Clark, W.K. • *The History of the S.P.C.K.* (London: SPCK, 1959).

Luther, Martin • 'The Right and Power of a Christian Congregation or Community to Judge all Teaching and to call, appoint, and dismiss Teachers, established and proved from Scripture' (1523), in *Luther's Works* (55 vols; Philadelphia: Fortress, 1970), vol. 39, 305–314.

McGillion, C. • *The Chosen Ones. The Politics of salvation in the Anglican Church* (Sydney: Allen & Unwin, 2005).

McNeil, S. • 'Body Image: Ecclesiology and Governance in Changing Times', in Kaye, *'Wonderful and Confessedly Strange'*, 201–221.

Micklem, P.A. • *Australia's First Bishop. A Brief Memoir of William Grant Broughton* (Sydney: Angus & Robertson, 1936).

Neil, C., & J.M. Willoughby (eds.), • *The Tutorial Prayer Book. For the Teacher, the Student, and the General Reader* (London: Harrison Trust, [2]1913 [1912]).

Neill, S. • *Anglicanism* (London: Penguin, 1965).

O'Brien, P. T. • *The Letter to the Ephesians* (Grand Rapids: Eerdmans, 1999).

Peck, A.L. • *Anglicanism and Episcopacy. A Re-Examination of the Evidence* (London: Faith Press, 1958).

Pettegree, A. • *Foreign Protestant Communities in Sixteenth Century London* (Oxford: Clarendon, 1986).

Porter, M. • *The New Puritans. The Rise of Fundamentalism in the Anglican Church* (Melbourne: Melbourne University Press, 2006).

Rayner, K. • 'Historical and Global Contexts', in Kaye, *'Wonderful and Confessedly Strange'*, 21–44.

Reid, D. • 'Anglican Diversity and Conflict: A Case Study on God, Gender, and Authority', in Kaye, *'Wonderful and Confessedly Strange'*, 240–265.

Robinson, D.W.B. • 'Presidency and Assistance in Ministering Word and Sacrament: A Note'. Unpublished discussion paper presented to the Sydney Diocesan Doctrine Commission, 1996). Republished in P.G. Bolt and M.D. Thompson (eds.), *Donald Robinson. Selected Works* (Camperdown, NSW: ACR and Moore College 2008), Vol. 2, Ch. 32.

Robinson, D.W.B. • 'Ministry in the Anglican Formularies and in the New Testament' (Unpublished discussion paper presented to the Sydney Diocesan Doctrine Commission 1994).

Robinson, D. W. B. • 'Lay Presidency at the Lord's Supper: Another Point of View' (Unpublished discussion paper presented to the Sydney Diocesan Doctrine Commission 1994).

Robinson, D.W.B. • 'Quiet Revolution "Mistaken"', *Southern Cross* (October, 1999), 8.

Stibbs, A.M. • *Sacrament Sacrifice and Eucharist - The Meaning Function and Use of the Lord's Supper* (London: Tyndale Press, 1961).

Stott, J. (ed.) • *The Anglican Communion and Scripture: papers from the First International Consultation of the Evangelical Fellowship in the Anglican Communion, Canterbury, UK, June 1993* (Oxford: Regnum, 1996).

Sykes, N. • *Old Priest and New Presbyter. The Anglican Attitude to Episcopacy, Presbyterianism and Papacy since the Reformation* (Cambridge: Cambridge University Press, 1956).

Synge, F.C. • 'The Challenge of the Frontiers', in *Anglican Congress 1963: Report of Proceedings* (Toronto: Editorial Committee, 1963), 155–64.

Taylor, Nicholas • *Lay Presidency at the Eucharist: An Anglican Approach* (London: T. & T. Clark, 2009). A pre-publication version was kindly made available by the author.

Tertullian • *Tertullian's Treatises on Marriage and Remarriage. To His Wife. An Exhortation to Chastity. Monogamy* (ACW 13; W.P. Le Saint, transl.; London: Longmans, Green & Co, 1961).

Tertullian • *Tertullian's Homily on Baptism* (E. Evans, ed. & transl.; London: SPCK, 1964).

Woodhouse, J.W. • 'Lay Administration of the Lord's Supper: A Change to Stay the Same', Speech to Sydney Synod, October 1994; now published as Chapter 1 in this volume.

Woodhouse, J.W • '"Lay Presidency" at the Lord's Supper: A reply to Archbishop Carnley's Response to the Report of the Sydney Diocesan Doctrine Commission' (Unpublished discussion paper presented to the Sydney Diocesan Doctrine Commission, 1994).

c. Legal Cases

Arches Court, May 31, 1844, *Titchmarsh v Chapman.*

Wylde v Attorney General (NSW) (1948) 78 CLR 224.

d. Websites & Webpages

http://www.anglican.org.au/docs/Canon%201998-13%20Services.pdf.

http://www.anglican.org.au/docs/ATWomenBishop270907.pdf.

http://www.anglican.org.au/docs/Proceedings2004master.pdf.

http://www.anglican.org.au/governance.cfm?SID=25&SSID=156&PID=282.

http://www.anglican.org.au/index.cfm?SID=2&SSID=6.

http://www.anglican.org.au/index.cfm?SID=2&SSID=5&PID=6.

http://www.archbishopofcanterbury.org/media/pdf/n/0/Lambeth_20opening_20address.pdf.

http://www.domlife.org/2007Stories/church_MinstryResponseDUTCH.html.

http://www.gafcon.org/index.php?option=com_content&task=view&id=79&Itemid=31.

http://history.hanover.edu/texts/engref/er80.html.

http://www.lambethconference.org/1998/news/acnspast.cfm.

http://www.lambethconference.org/daily/news.cfm/2008/7/29/ACNS4487.

http://www.lambethconference.org/lc2008/news/news.cfm?mode=entry&entry=0EF2A68
4-EE2D-9FA2-F5CAA03F0133AE3E.

http://www.lambethconference.org/resolutions/downloads/1930.pdf.

http://www.liturgy.co.nz/worship/matters_files/dutchdominicans.html;

http://www.reform-ireland.org.uk/layceleb.htm.

http://www.sds.asn.au/Site/100818.asp?ph=sy.